Apartment Syndication
Made Easy
A Step by Step Guide

My Journey from $7 to $250 Million

Vinney (Smile) Chopra
U.S. Commercial Investing Champion

Dedication

I would like to dedicate this book to Kanchan, my wife, and Neil and Monica, our two great children who have encouraged and motivated me all my life to excel in every endeavor I took on. Also to my Uncle Om, who gave me the opportunity to come to USA to pursue my dream and to my teachers, mentors, relatives, thousands of friends and my mastermind students who inspire me daily.

I have always believed and lived by this quote
"I have always believed in an individual's ability to shape the world around them through positive thought and selfless actions"
—Vinney (Smile) Chopra

Table of Contents

Introduction to Commercial Syndication

Got $7?

Then you've got an opportunity, but NOT in the way you might expect and NOT in the sense of being able to buy two gallons of gas or two lattes at the coffee shop or that slice of dessert after dinner. No, you have a REAL opportunity!

Relax! There's NO sales pitch or product coming. I'm not after your $7. Instead, I'd like to share a story. A story of what's possible. A story of how far you can actually go starting out with just $7 in your pocket.

The story, by the way, is my own. Since we have yet to meet, allow me to introduce myself. My name is **Vinney "Smile" Chopra**. I'm the author of this book and a real estate investor. You may not be able to tell, but I'm smiling right now! In fact, I'm perpetually smiling. Of course, Smile is not legally my middle name, but it is what those who meet me soon start to call me. Why the smile? Well, why not? After all, smiling is supposed to be good for your health. Beyond that, though, I'm 'all smiles' because of how far I have come in the last forty years. That's the story I want to share with you on the pages ahead.

It's the story of how I came to the United States, from India, in the 1970's, with just $7 in my pocket. Oh! Don't worry! It isn't a sad story. Let's just say I earned "a few more dollars" along the way, arriving at a point today where a bottle of Coke, though I do still enjoy drinking one, is no longer the "luxury" it once was.

Goodness! Has it really been that long? Pardon me while I reminisce. Forty years since I stood there. Fresh off the plane in New York City. Dehydrated by jet lag. Struggling as my body switched to NYC's climate - a drastic change from what I was accustomed to in India. And craving more than anything a bottle of Coke sitting in a glass case at a restaurant. It might as well have been a diamond on display at the museum. I could not afford it - not at the $2 it cost.

Oh yes, right! We're not sharing a sad story here! How things can change for the better! In my case, that change meant going from a $2 Coke being a "luxury" to acquiring over $250 million in multifamily real estate assets. That's right!

How? Multifamily real estate! It's what I do!

If that word "multifamily" doesn't ring a bell, it has to do with real estate relating to apartment buildings. Simply put, as a multifamily real estate investor, I invest in apartment buildings and enjoy helping others do the same.

More specifically, I lead groups of investors in what are called "**syndications.**" Though I'll share a more inclusive definition of syndication in a few pages, what it means is that I raise money from investors to acquire apartment properties, manage and add value to those properties, and then sell the properties later for a profit.

To date, I have led more than 26 syndications and amassed a portfolio of over 3,000 units (i.e. individual apartments). As I write, I am in the capital raising process of my largest offering to date (#27), and it stands to provide me with a HUGE RAISE. My biggest one returned $50 Million in Equity, a success about which I am excited and proud! With this raise, my investors and I will be able to add approximately $300 Million worth of more multifamily acquisitions. Well, as I am sending this book to be published, I have great news that should reinforce your commitment to learning a lot in the chapters ahead where I will discuss so many tricks of the trade. You might ask, what is the good news? Well, I just got the largest mutifamily 324 units under contract with my half partners (great syndicators also) worth $52 million in a superb emerging market. Are you excited yet?

> *"The success doesn't come overnight."*

The story behind my success in real estate investment and syndication is interwoven with the stories of success for others, including families, colleagues, and my staff. I have always followed and give testament to the power of four incredible words: ENTHUSIASM; PASSION; PERSISTENCE; and POSITIVITY!

Let's talk about that last one. The positive attitude plays an important role in anyone's life. Negativity is viral, breeding negative energy here and there. If we are not cautious, those negative factors will penetrate our thoughts and minds. So, I believe we should really shield ourselves from this disease, refusing to let it contaminate our minds, our speech, and our attitudes. Instead, I promote being positive - keeping happiness in our thoughts, exuding joy in our smiles, and doing as much good as we can for the people around us. It is a simple approach, but by adopting it, we will do well. That has been my #1 goal in life.

Why do I mention this now? Two reasons.

First, it helps you in understanding who I am and what I do.

Secondly, and arguably, more importantly, applying this principle of positivity is really what can make that $7 we were talking about earlier so much more powerful.

If you will really think about it, you have a lot going for you since you probably do have at least $7 in your pocket. So maybe it is not literally in your pocket at this precise moment (since hardly anyone carries cash these days), but chances are you do have at least $7 in your bank account or somewhere.

For others, depending on your profession, you may have substantially more than $7 right now. Maybe you are in the medical, legal, or financial profession, or perhaps you are enjoying success in another line of work. Maybe you are what they call a "high net worth individual." Maybe you have enough money to buy your own Coke machine rather than just a single bottle. Or maybe you own stock in Coca-Cola. So, $7 does not seem that much to you.

Regardless, $7 (and I keep saying this) IS MORE THAN ENOUGH!

Enough Single-family?

Great question! I realize I haven't been clear on that.

By "enough" I mean enough money to become financially independent. Where you are able to live comfortably at the level you desire, funding your lifestyle with recurring cash flow, you are a financially independent person. **Financial independence** also means you have enough wealth on which to live without working. **Financially independent** people have assets that generate income (cash flow) that is at least equal to their expenses.

How do you create such a cash flow?

In the same way, I have, with multifamily real estate. So, you, too, will be buying small and large apartment buildings, managing and adding value to those buildings, and then, potentially, selling them for a substantial profit.

Think you're up to the task?

Feel free to say "No." In fact, at this point, I would not blame you if you did because there is this ONE BIG thing we haven't talked about - the proverbial ELEPHANT in the room. And where buying apartment buildings is concerned, this ELEPHANT is HUGE! The elephant is, of course, MONEY! Or, rather, a lack of it.

Most likely, you don't have a few million dollars just lying around that you can use to run out and buy a commercial building or an apartment building. So, how is it even possible to think of making such an expensive purchase or acquisition? You need money, but WHERE would you get it? I'm so glad you asked! You can get it through SYNDICATION!

Now, I'm almost certain of your next question: What is syndication?

SYNDICATION. Though we mentioned it briefly a page or so ago, let's make it very clear by formally defining the concept. **Syndication**, as it applies to multifamily real estate is **the process of pooling money from other people with very little money of your own to purchase an asset that, perhaps, none of you might be able to acquire individually.**

This is very much the same concept, I believe, of what many of the wealthy individuals and corporations that have become so successful in the marketplace have done. You see tech startups and major hedge funds raising private equity all the time to create massive wealth for both their corporation and their individual investors. Why not apply the same concept to your venture? I have, and it works!

In the pages that follow, I will share with you ways in which you are able to leverage those same wealth-building strategies, on a smaller scale, to realize your dream and place yourself in complete control of your financial future. I will confess that I always thought that building a business using "other people's money" did not go past late-night info-mercials. My own experience, though, has led me to realize that it is not about me building a business with someone else's money as much as it is about creating opportunity and, along the way, helping a lot of other people whose lack of time limits their investment options.

Thinking back to our new term, syndication, you will remember that it is the pooling together of money from groups of investors. Quite simply, syndication will allow you to raise money to buy nearly any apartment building(s) you desire and then to use those buildings to achieve your own financial independence!

> *Success will not be handed to you today, get up,*
> *get out and put in the work; do what is necessary*
> *and then enjoy the sweet taste of victory.*

It won't be easy, though. At least not initially. For there is a lot to learn.

When I say that, I am still speaking from experience. You see, the success I've obtained through syndication - those 26 (soon 27, in 45 days, the due diligence was finished last week- as we close on this new asset) deals - has only come through tireless effort and ongoing education, through trial and error, through collaborative endeavor and collective patience with team members as we have endured the daily grind to find the solutions to the challenges along the way. Through it all, though, we have maintained that positive attitude that has fueled our motivation to continually move forward. If you, too, are willing to put in the work and educate yourself in the practice, there really is no limit to your ability to find success in syndications. You could soon have as many of your own as I have, and hopefully more.

The key is effort and education. You, personally, will have to put in the effort. I can't do that for you. What I can help you with, however, is the education. And frankly, I'm happy to do so. It's actually the reason I've written this book - the one you're reading right now. And the fact that you are reading it is an indication that you are already serious about educating yourself in this process.

This book was born out of my dismay over the lack of resources detailing exactly how to work systematically- Step by Step to form great syndications to invest in commercial real estate. I say "dismay" because it is startling to me that such a powerful strategy like syndication is just not discussed in any depth, especially when you think of how useful this strategy can be in helping people finally invest in commercial assets like apartment buildings, office buildings, strip shopping centers, hotels or even in large scale flipping and wholesaling, thus securing their financial independence.

You might appreciate knowing, before we move on, that I realized in 2004, after investing in rentals and flipping houses for almost 20 years, that I was not in a position to build wealth rapidly simply because those real estate efforts were not going to be a viable path to creating wealth since those investments were not scalable.

So, why aren't there any good books out there on the "nuts and bolts" of doing a syndication deal? Your guess is as good as mine. What we can both be sure of, though, is that this book will teach you those "nuts and bolts." In the pages ahead in simple terms, you will be learning **exactly** - and I do mean, exactly - how to do your syndication deals.

To keep things clear in your mind, our discussion of syndications will be based around a fun analogy of spinning five plates.

Picture in your mind what that looks like. Imagine a person balancing those five spinning plates, carefully keeping them all in motion at once while not dropping a single one. It is, quite literally, a balancing act that requires the utmost care and attention. After all, if the person spinning those plates slips up in any way, they may lose control of all the plates resulting in a mess on the floor - with the plates shattered into pieces and strewn everywhere.

See the parallels now to syndications? The same care and attention are required in syndications, too. In this latter case, failure to properly manage all aspects of a syndication - each of those five plates - can also result in a mess (may I suggest "shattered dream"?). And with syndications, that mess can be decidedly worse too. So, in place of broken plates, for example, you'd be looking at the brokenness of lawsuits, financial losses, and irreparable damage to your reputation with valued investors, real estate brokers, and countless other teams (legal and lending).

Relax and breathe now, though, and rest assured that you will soon be adept at spinning those five "plates." Consider this my promise to you as we look toward the upcoming chapters: By the end of this book, you will be knowledgeable enough to confidently "spin the plates" and accomplish your first syndication deal. To set the stage for this "Five Plates" concept, I will use the next several chapters to speak specifically about multifamily real estate and syndication.

To give you a sense of what each "plate" entails - here is a preview of them, one by one...

Plate #1 - Building Superb Teams

This first plate will guide you in building a team of people to assist you on each real estate deal that you perform. Building a team is essential, both for negotiating the deals, themselves and for feeling confident in your practice.

On that second point, understand that having the right team will give you unbelievable confidence when talking to investors. You will be able to boldly look investors in the eye and tell them assuredly about the high returns you will be delivering in a syndication deal. Your confidence will come from the fact that you have a high-quality team in place to manage the various aspects of the investment.

To gain such confidence, you will need to build your team. And that is what we will cover in the chapter about the first plate. As you read that chapter, you will learn how to find and assemble the key players in your team, including brokers, contractors, attorneys, property managers, and building inspectors (for due diligence).

Plate #2 - Building Investor Lists and Relationships

Our next plate is also related to finding the right people for your syndications. In this case, those people will be investors.

How do you find investors and ultimately close deals with them?

There's a right way to do it, along with plenty of wrong ways. Having seen many "would-be" syndicators do it the wrong way, I want to help you avoid their mistakes. So, with this second plate, I will be sharing my personal strategies on how to successfully interact with investors. These strategies have helped me and the countless students I have coached over the years amass successes instead of failures. As you read Plate #2, and then administer your deal(s) later on, you will, undoubtedly, find the strategies to be just as helpful.

Plate #3 - Underwriting and Analyzing the Deals

If there is one area in which the students I have coached often become overwhelmed, it is in the concept and process of underwriting. Students frequently feel intimidated by the amount of calculations that must be performed when "running the numbers" (underwriting) a deal. They realize that underwriting is essential to know whether or not a deal really makes sense as an investment. Yet, handling all of those computations, especially if you're NOT a mathematician or a mechanical engineer, can be a daunting task - one from which many will be tempted to shy away.

Even if you do enjoy and excel in math, how do you keep underwriting from holding you back - so that you don't drown in models and never get started? You do it, in the same way, I advise my students. You will discover that method, as well, as we cover Plate #3 on underwriting.

Plate #4 - Loan Qualification

"Money doesn't grow on trees," as the expression goes. Instead, it often comes as a result of loans. Yet the process of obtaining the loans can be difficult and complicated. And, of course, they must be repayable.

That's where Plate #4 comes in. We will be covering all you need to know about securing the right loans for your syndicated real estate deals. Key aspects of this, to be covered, including finding a capable loan broker, structuring your financing for a deal in the right way, and forming the right legal entities for the overall syndication.

Plate #5 - Property Take Over
and Management Team

Last but not least, we will spin Plate #5 on property takeover and your management team. This final plate marks the last essential aspect of accomplishing a syndication.

You can think of it then as "home plate" like in baseball or in cricket (where I'm from in India). Having "run the bases" with Plates #1, #2, #3, and #4, you are now ready to "bring it home" with Plate #5. Plate #5 will help you ensure each syndication you facilitate is indeed a "home run!"- satisfying you, your investors, and every other player on your team.

To guarantee you score that "home run," Plate #5 will cover what to do on the day of closing when you and your investors assume ownership (takeover) of the property you have acquired. You will be learning what to do, along with how to maintain the property using a management team later on.

How does all that sound? Ready to dive into this whole "syndication" thing?

Before we do, there are three last-minute items we need to cover.

One relates to motivation.

Given the motivational message and encouraging tone of this book, you should be aware of my track record as a motivational speaker. To date, I have given over 10,000 speeches aimed at meeting life's challenges with positive thinking and setting goals of personal success. So, when you hear, throughout this book, my "you can do it" messages - understand that I mean it. Motivation is one of those things about which I am quite passionate; it is kind of a way of life for me.

Secondly, I need to tell you about my two "past lives."

Before I began my career in Real Estate Investing (REI), I was as a mechanical engineer. This experience gave me a skill which is essential for success, both in engineering and in nearly any other pursuit. The skill to which I am I'm referring is the ability to design and implement systems. In the context of engineering, systems are what allow a plane to stabilize its motion - despite gusts of wind. They are what cause a robotic arm to move in time with other aspects of a manufacturing line.

Looking beyond engineering and on to countless other areas of life, you will see systems at work. Indeed, it seems that there is no "safe" zone that is free from the benefits of implementing systems. Fortunately for us, systems are particularly suited for real estate investing. This is because of how much time and attention is required to facilitate a real estate deal. To save time, without dropping any of the five plates in a syndication, it is absolutely necessary to have a well-designed system or two (or ten)!

Creating a system may sound like an insurmountable challenge right now, and you may not even yet know what such a system would look like. Don't worry. With my background as both an engineer and a Real Estate professional, you are in good hands. I promise not to leave you to figure out systems for yourself. Instead, I will provide lots of guidance over the course of this text on those very systems. After all, my goal in sharing this book with you is to provide you with a clear understanding of what I have done with systems in REI so that you can go out and build your own.

Alright, that's my first "past life." Before that, I was as a door-to-door salesperson - selling cookbooks, Bibles, and children's books.

A salesperson!!!! Right, they're the bad guys, I know. The pests who knock on your door, interrupting dinner or family time. Look, I get it. Salespeople are often synonymous with the devil... even if they are selling Bibles!

So, I mention that past as a salesman to you little reluctantly. I do, however, think it is important for you to be aware of this experience since sales is essential to raising money in a syndication. And it was, in many ways, through that sales experience going door to door to earn my way through college that I learned the basic skills of selling a product and closing the deal, two skills that are essential to this business of syndications.

Perhaps, having done my time in sales, I can hopefully save you from having to do the same. No need for you to go door-to-door for three summers, as I did, selling books in Georgia, Virginia and South Carolina. You can shortcut the process by hearing my tips here, which come from the sales world and have been adapted for REI and syndications.

The final thing I want to mention now, among our last-minute items is where to find me. That's important because as exhaustive as this book will be on syndications, you will probably want to know even more about the process, about who I am, or about what is covered in this book.

Here's How:

Weekly as of this writing, I host a Facebook Live event. It takes place every Friday at 10:00 AM (Pacific Time, PST), and I answer questions on all things related to multifamily syndication investing and management. I would like to personally invite you to attend!

In the same way, you are also welcomed to check out my website (VinneyChopra.com) and my Multifamily Syndication Academy (MultifamilySyndicationAcademy.com) or Multifamily Academy (MultifamilyAcademy.com).

Together all those resources (the event, my sites, the academy) will help you beyond what's in this book. I provide personal coaching & group mentoring to students who are serious about becoming multifamily real estate investors and rock stars!

I humbly offer this content to you, as my students often comment about the great content they have learned in the lectures and courses found throughout these three resources. Just a few kind words from a few of my students are:

"Vinney's Multifamily Syndication Academy has been amazing! I would've never dreamed that I could sit with Investors and thoroughly explain the benefits of investing in a Multifamily Deal, much less have the knowledge of how to structure a Syndication Fund. Now, After a few short months, I am able to find a deal, research the area, underwrite and go through all of the steps of putting together a great deal with little help from our mastermind group.

If you're interested in getting started, or stepping up your game, in Multifamily Syndication, Vinney's Multifamily Syndication Academy is amazing!

All of the materials you need are provided. You are not left starving for information or asked to pay for any extra courses. It is all there, ready and available when you need it.

Vinney is a great coach and mentor!"

– Daniel C

"Vinney Chopra is one of the most knowledgeable and generous mentors in the Multifamily Syndication space. His experience is invaluable and he is willing and generous with that knowledge and experience in his teaching and mentoring. IMO he is the best single source for this type of information to be found anywhere. Vinney is open, kind resourceful and has a genuine interest in his pupils succeeding. He is a true believer in "paying it forward" and so his success become contagious! He is the BEST!"

– Stephen D

"Two years ago, I found myself working as a sales manager 65 hours a week and I could not figure out how I could break free of the golden handcuffs. Once I learned about the power of MultiFamily Syndication I knew it was something I wanted to get involved with, I just did not know how I would do it. To this day, I think I may still be there had I not met Vinney. Coaching with Vinney and going through his Multi-Family Syndication Academy given me the fundamental education I needed to close my first deal and quit my job. Today I have invested in/control 300 units and have another 240 under contact as I write this. Vinney takes what seems to be as he calls it a "10,000 lb gorilla" and breaks it into simple actionable steps using his philosophy of spinning the plates. The best part about Vinney is the fact that he leads by example as a true veteran in the field, who has worn every hat including acquisitions, dispositions, asset management, property management, and more. You name it, he has done it. Thank you, Vinney."

– Dylan M

"Vinney has changed the way I look at investing in Real Estate! By joining his Academy, he breaks down the syndication model to 5 spinning plates and teaches us the importance of keeping focused. He is not only a teacher but an inspiration for me to achieve my goals. Thanks Vinney, I have learned soooo much from you."

– Sheldon K

"Three months ago, I knew nothing about real estate and now after taking Vinney's courses I am extremely knowledgeable on how to analyze and buy huge apartment buildings. If you are the type of person who is looking to increase their wealth and achieve financial independence, multifamily real estate is the right choice for you. Vinney has some of the best industry experience by owning and managing over $250M in Real Estate and managing over 3,500 units. He personally teaches his classes, answers everybody's questions, and is extremely transparent with how he runs his business, his properties, and even partners with students if they have great deals! He is extremely motivational and pushes his students to try to become more successful than him. If you are serious about building your real estate portfolio and want to learn from the best then Vinney is your guy!"

– Rohun J

Now, let's return to our discussion of syndication. As you recall, I promised you that we were going to talk in depth on the subject. And I will remain true to my word as we move on to the first of those five figurative plates you will soon be spinning as a syndicator.

Before we get down to the nitty-gritty, though, and move on to our discussion of Plate #1, let me leave you with a saying which epitomizes all we will be discussing. It comes from Tony Robbins, a man who is among the source of some of my greatest inspiration. In a big way, his motivational words were instrumental in helping me go from $7 to where I am today. Perhaps you, too, have been inspired by Tony. If so, you might recognize this quintessential quote, which ties, I believe, perfectly to the overall concept of team-building and syndication.

Resources are NEVER the problem. It's a lack of resourcefulness.

Think about that quote for a moment. Let it sink in! Now, as we move forward together, consider it as we determine how you can be resourceful in overcoming any lack of financial resources to enter REI.

Then join me in the next chapter as we get resourceful in building your team for your future in Commercial/Multifamily Syndications...I want to emphasize that we can syndicate to raise money to purchase any kind of assets in real estate, residential flipping, wholesaling, offices, Industrial, hotels, shopping centers or multifamily (apartments). I chose the last sector because it made more sense to me with lesser risks and big rewards at starting of my journey. And it's still true after 15 years of being in it.

CHAPTER ONE

Why Syndication?

This is the very essence of this book, Why Syndication? To be fair, though, we should begin by answering what is syndication?

Real estate syndication is an effective way for investors to pool their financial and intellectual resources to invest in properties and projects much bigger than they could afford or manage on their own. In other words, **syndication is a group investment**. I like to say it this way: Syndication is when more than one person entrusts you with his or her money by investing in your deal. Simply put, it is a group of like-minded investors that pool their money together in order to participate in investment opportunities that no single one of them would likely handle individually. Although real estate syndication has been around for decades, until recently (and before the advent of crowdfunding), syndicated investments were difficult for individual investors to access. Thankfully, this is no longer the case.

> *"Two is better than one because they have a good return for their labor..."*
> – *King Solomon of Israel (from the book of Ecclesiastes)*
>
> *"Two heads are better than one."*
> – *Old English Proverb (John Heywood, 1546)*

When investors decide to syndicate, each has his or her own interests. One may contribute financial support only and take a passive role, while some others may decide to contribute more than that. It is common, not uncommon to see some members of the syndicate take an active role in the business by directing the affairs of the investment either explicitly or through their suggestions and guidance often adding to the deal the strong qualities of confidence and experience. This gives investors with a limited financial power the ability to have a stake in a big investment that they previously thought to be exclusively reserved for wealthy investors.

Who can invest in a syndication deal? Well, anyone! Consider the points below that address the reasons investors choose to participate in syndication, and you will see that a good syndication is attractive to a wide array of individuals from a broad spectrum of lifestyles and socio-economic circumstances.

Why Do Investors Practice Syndication?

As you make note of the variety of individuals who could find themselves part of the deal, consider the three major reasons people choose to buy into this type of investment idea.

1. **Lack of experience**: You are wealthy and can afford to purchase an expensive property. Unfortunately, you are lacking the experience to make such large investments. Don't worry! To be on the safe side, now you can decide to form an alliance with others to finance the project with investors with greater degrees of experience.

   There are, literally, countless individuals who would love to invest in real estate. You may be one of them, thus you are reading this book. Those potential investors want very much to loan their money to someone like me (or you), syndicators who will profitably nest it for them and provide good returns as passive income. Most of these investors know a good deal when they see one, and regardless of the level of capital they can use to pursue it, there is a place for them in the deal when the money is pooled together. Syndication becomes the viable solution for many potential or experienced investors.

2. **Limited financial resources:** You are interested in real estate investments, but you do not possess the capital to go buy the piece of real estate that is sure to turn a profit. Most syndicates consider including investors with shallower pockets from which to invest in their efforts to raise the capital needed for a big property with a hefty price tag. Instead of leaving the property at the mercy of wealthy investors, individual real estate managers may decide to pool their resources together and acquire the property.

3. **Lack of time**: You are a busy doctor, lawyer, accountant, engineer, teacher, or some other type of professional, and you have the money to invest in real estate but not the time to do so. Some business people may also be interested in diversifying their investment to include real estate. Passive membership of the syndicate may appeal to you. The lack of time and working knowledge of the business will necessitate pooling resources with a syndicate to realize their dreams of becoming a property owner.

The Nuts and Bolts of a Syndication

The group of investors is usually headed by a syndicator. The syndicator has multiple responsibilities of managing, organizing, planning, producing, and representing the syndicate in all business and legal dealings. Either an individual or a corporation may be appointed to take on this role. In most cases, the syndicator is an accountant, an engineer, a real estate broker, or an attorney specializing in real estate law. Although the role of syndicator is not exclusive to these types of professionals, the experience garnered in these lines of duty will be useful in navigating the difficult terrain of real estate investment.

Are you dreaming of investing in real estate? Get started with syndication!

Why should I practice syndication?

Now that we know what syndication is, let's answer the why! There must be some advantages and benefits to this form or real estate investing, right?!? Of course, there are! Syndication has a lot of benefits that makes it appealing to many investors. Some of these benefits are discussed below.

The syndicator is a specialist

The syndication team is led by an experienced real estate professional or other skilled professionals in a related field. This individual brings to the deal a wealth of knowledge and expertise. So, the whole team will benefit. This will be instrumental to driving the team towards realizing the goals and objectives of the group. If you are just getting started, do not be intimidated - you can be the syndicator with the right learning mindset, approach, and discipline!

It facilitates the acquisition of larger properties

The investors have the financial power to buy bigger properties due to the large sum of money that will be contributed towards that goal by the score's investors involved. Where an individual investor may give up on an investment if it becomes too expensive to personally finance, the exact inverse is the case for syndicated investments.

Investors can make a monthly profit from their investment

If the syndicate has a property that can be rented, the syndicate will benefit from the monthly income from the property. Each member of the syndicate will be paid according to the agreement signed when the syndicate was formed. The monthly income is one big advantage that members of a syndicate find attractive.

It encourages diversification

Syndication helps an investor with little funds spread his resources across different properties. He can also purchase a big property with the support of other investors. When the members of the syndicate pool their resources together, each member will be entitled to diversified investment, which will eventually translate into a steady income.

That is a welcome idea for investors as their money will not be tied down to a single investment.

It provides cash reserves

The ability to remain in business and build wealth is one of the most influential factors for a potential investor. Syndication affords investors the access to sufficient capital that can be used to invest further or can be used to boost the financial value of a property, yielding resistance to economic crisis or downturn.

It safeguards investors against significant losses

An individual investor is always potentially at the risk of losing most of his or her investment if a deal goes bad. The members of a syndicate are immune to such a great loss since they all contribute to the project. Any losses incurred will be shared by all of the members, taking the weight of a great loss from the shoulders of any single investor.

It is affordable

Pooling resources with others have a financial benefit attached to it. While individual investors may find it difficult to make a large impressive down payment, a syndicate can easily do this and make the best use of their capital to increase their returns. This will help all involved to save cost and increase profit. Whatever the syndicate saves from their different investments will be available for the members to share, adding to individual profit from the investment.

Syndicated expertise is superior expertise

It is much wiser for investors to leverage their collective expertise than for a single investor to stake everything on their own personal opinion when making decisions. The wealth of experience and skill of the group will be invaluable, and the syndicate is sure to fare better by implementing some policies that are drawn from this combined effort. Real estate is a bit more complex than most people think. It requires skills to determine the real value of a property, negotiate purchase agreements, define lease terms, finance a purchase, or manage a property. Having multiple individuals with a variety of skills will make it easier to handle the different aspects of real estate.

Revenue is predictable

You can derive a reliable income from syndication through rents or income from leased properties. If you have a strong and experienced management team, you can work towards getting the best tenants for your properties. Through the rents you get from these tenants, you will have a regular monthly income from your investment.

Your capital appreciates

Syndication allows you of capital appreciation when the assets are bought in good job growth markets. If you and your team can ensure proper maintenance of the property, the property's value will perpetually increase. This will mean increased rents from tenants and increased occupancy rates if the property is leased out.

This will automatically mean a steady appreciation of your capital.

Overall returns are healthy

Most of the time if the syndication sponsor is knowledgeable and organized with the best foundations of taking care of investors and residents or tenants in commercial buildings a syndication will go as planned. The ability to leverage the syndicate to acquire multifamily property will guarantee you very healthy overall returns. You will get a stable income from rents and capital gains as a result of an increase in the value of a property. If you have a very effective cash flow structure, you will save on taxes. The result is a good overall return on your investment.

You have a tangible asset

Investing in real estate is interesting, especially if you are a part of a syndicate and have access to enough funds to go after good properties. While people trading in stocks and bonds are subjected to the fear of fluctuation, you have no such fear because you have a tangible asset that guarantees you passive income regularly. The return on investment remains quite good even when the economy is bad.

You are protected from liability

Unlike other high-risks investments, a syndication gives you steady income without subjecting you to the challenge associated with other types of investment. You are not exposed to unnecessary risks or to shouldering any liability from your partnership in the business. While the income is good, the management is responsible for running the business, and any liability from the business is a collective liability and not a personal one. This makes it easy to bear problems and to solve them. Therefore, no matter what happens to the property, you are well shielded from any personal responsibility.

When answering the question, **"Why Syndicate**?" the reasons are plentiful as you can see. So, let's tackle one more related question: How do you get started in multifamily syndication? Starting a real estate syndicate requires recruiting people who are ready to commit their financial support. Many considerations are involved.

Real Estate Syndication Groups

1. Limited Partners: Partners or money investors

2. General Partners: The experts or managers

Real estate syndication is interwoven with two groups of people: partners or money investors and the experts or managers in this field. Money investors are considered, in this business, the limited partners or LPs. The experts or managers are known as general partners or GPs. The two groups play complementary roles to make the syndicate a success. While the money partners contribute to the capital, the general partners are responsible for the running of the syndicate. They have the desired experience to manage a syndicate to achieve the objectives to which they are committed.

How to Start a Real Estate Syndicate

The LP group may consist of many investors, sometimes, hundreds of them, with individual investments that can often range between $5,000 and $500,000. The money is turned over to the GP with the experience to conduct other aspects of the business, such as purchasing the property, managing it, and reselling the property at the right time.

Basically, investors are pooling their capital together and becoming part of something bigger than they could do on their own and can participate with a syndicator who has knowledge of that industry. An investor can use that for their investment to generate a return instead of going it alone with limited knowledge and funds. This highlights the importance of having some members among the syndicate who are experienced in the field.

Finding the Right Syndicate

Finding the best syndicate will be the most difficult aspect of syndication. Think of it as a challenge, though, rather than a problem. It really is quite possible if you make the necessary effort. Extensive research and diligence will be required in this process so that you will have enough information about potential members from which to choose. Don't forget, you are not looking for money partners only; you are also looking for an expert in the niche. Honest, experienced with great track records and with the highest passion to help others. The importance of getting the right people involved is best summarized by Thomas Beyer, president of Prestigious Properties Group Corp.

> *"Too often four guys with money who know each other profes-*
> *sionally pool their money, but someone has to spend the time to*
> *research the market and location, find a suitable asset, negoti-*
> *ate the price, terms, and conditions, find a suitable mortgage*
> *and property manager, than to constantly monitor everything.*
> *All this takes time and expertise usually gained over the years*
> *and exceeds the expertise of an average guy with money."*
>
> *– Thomas Beyer, President*
> *Prestigious Properties Group Corp.*

Don't forget this important point when assembling the members of your syndicate. That will give you both the financial power and the experience that will help you sail through the stormy real estate world. And think of the benefits that are found in the great opportunities you will have to work with other real estate investors!

Effective Syndication

Syndication has never been an easy task. But if you practice my five steps of syndication, I believe you will find it to be well worth the effort as you look toward a truly amazing future.

Start up with creating the best team! This team will consist of RE brokers, mortgage brokers, contractors, a due diligence team, legal (RE & syndication) counsel, and management companies. Selecting the best partners is essential in the real estate sector. It is imperative that we build a strong relationship with many brokers in the designated "emerging market." For a great syndicator, it is vital that the market in which you are buying be a strong, emerging market where the investors' money will flow in easily and quickly. So, as a first step in creating your team, go ahead and seek out a high net-worth individual or one who is experienced in the commercial real estate market. He or she will be an invaluable asset and resource.

1. **Build a list of investors**, and then build your relationship with them by softening, educating, and feeding them with information through monthly newsletters and personalized emails. Along the way, don't ever stop educating them about the benefits of Multifamily investing, how to do it, and the emerging market trends. The more they know, the stronger your syndication team becomes. Teach your investors how to use their retirement funds via self-directed accounts. Inspire them with your message about why they should be ready to jump in at the right opportunity. Stress the importance of timing in syndication. First come–first served, is the basic theory in this sector!

We have designed a great plan: We pay 1.5-2% annual interest on the funds from investors beginning immediately after filling out the proper paperwork, getting accepted by us and wiring of their funds into the LLC bank account. Make sure you don't commingle, the funds from the investors need to go into the LLC bank account that will be purchasing the asset. You can only "break the funds"- take any money out to use for expenses or earnest money or any other thing only after meeting the minimum raise limit. The interest is paid from the day of deposit until the closing date of the acquisition. Our investors are satisfied with this great feature that I started 8 years back. I have shared this idea with thousands and it totally makes sense and fortunately, I have never lost my sleep or got stressed out before the final closing date due to lack of funds in the bank account for an on-time closing. I want to emphasize here that we must make the right choices in choosing the suitable and able investors who will have sufficient funds to invest. Please don't spend time and energy chasing wrong investors and flaky individuals.

Don't forget to ask for referrals and meet them personally. Conduct webinars. Attend RE and REI meetings, meetup groups, Toastmasters clubs, Chambers of Commerce, Wealth Groups and Clubs and other philanthropic organizations. Seek involvement where high net worth members gather. If the investors don't show up to dance with you at the closing, there is no deal at all! So, we must cultivate and nurture our relationships with investors. They are gold!!! Or perhaps they just have some gold! Either way, we need them! I am very happy to report that in my two acquisition companies we have 100% record of closing the 26 apartments purchases from LOI (letter of intent) stage to the finish line (successful closing).

2. Aggressively seek underwriting to find the "golden opportunity."

Get lots of off-market, on market deals, Operating Memorandums (OM) from brokers' offerings and learn the materials well. Just fill out the confidentiality agreements (CA)– practice, practice, practice! You will quickly become an amazing underwriter and also a successful syndicator. Become accomplished at the sampling and understanding of the tricks and rules of important market statistics like cash flows (CF), cash-on-cash returns (COC), net operating Income (NOI), internal rate of return (IRR), Return on Investment (ROI), and all other pertinent ratios.

3. Obtain Loan Qualification

A loan broker will guide you in this step to prepare your financial statement. Liquidity is a must for any investment. Discuss with your loan broker how to qualify for this investment. You may need to get a high net worth partner initially to qualify for the loan. You may find target seller financing to be an option, but this is rare. Usually, the net worth must equal or exceed the amount of the loan.

While in this process, it is important to also engage a great syndication attorney and/or a real estate attorney. Decide on the right entities and structures. You must establish total trust and confidence in this relationship. Research and hire a marketing company or virtual assistant to design the investor information packet. The Private Placement Memorandum (PPM), Operating Agreement (OA) and the Subscription Agreement (SA) and accompanying documents need to be prepared by a reputable syndication attorney. I will explain in details in Plate #4

4. Organize Your Property Take-over and Management Team

It is imperative to be fully prepared for the day of closing. This step is detailed and must happen smoothly. A decision needs to be made on whether to self-manage (like in all our acquisitions) or to hire a professional management company.

It is a challenge to find the very best, trustworthy, and professional company that can manage like you!! You must do a lot of inquiring and face to face interviewing to be able to ascertain which is the best fit for you.

The most important job of the syndicator is his or her fiduciary responsibilities to the valued investors since they have entrusted their life's savings to this syndication. The operation of the assets is the key to making sure that all the monthly or quarterly cash flows are generated from the operations of the properties and passed on to the investors regularly.

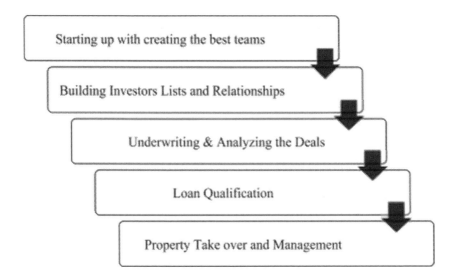

Starting up with creating the best teams

Building Investors Lists and Relationships

Underwriting & Analyzing the Deals

Loan Qualification

Property Take over and Management

What is a Security?

Hi, I wanted to talk a little bit about the security. As you know, in syndication, we are pulling the money together and we have to adhere to the laws of Securities and Exchange Commission. See, when somebody gives you money and they're entrusting you with their funds, so that you are overseeing the investment of the apartment or any business for profits, it's a security.

So, that's why we want to explain and you know, in this course you will find out a lot of great ideas. But again, I do want to say a disclaimer that I'm not an attorney, an LCC attorney or a CPA. I'm a broker, but I don't use my license to purchase the properties at all. I give the commissions to these listing agents and I'll share with you all my nuggets that I've done in all these, you know, 26 syndications and the 27th one coming up. As this book is going into publication, I know, so you will -- I just want to let you know that once we do a security, that is when somebody is entrusting their money to you then you have certain rules and regulations to follow. That's what we are able to crush together to understand them and then have the pre-existing relationship - that's another term, you will see. And also, accredited investors, sophisticated investors, suitable investors and we'll give you beautiful sites also of the syndication attorneys where you could go to and learn more about it too. So, we'll be able to do it slowly-slowly. Don't worry about it, but I just wanted to put that disclaimer.

Syndication Tips

This is why thousands of investors give investing in real estate as a member of a syndicate a shot. If you're seriously thinking about syndication, these tips will make you a millionaire.

1. Learn all you can about it!
This step is valid for anything worthwhile under the sun. You need to deepen your knowledge of syndication before proceeding to invest your time and money into it. It will become increasingly easier the more you know more about it. This raises the question; *how can you learn more about syndication?*

2. Do the research!
This is the simplest and best way to deepen your knowledge about syndication. Take time to know as much as possible about the topic by using all the resources at your disposal. The Internet is the best tool for conducting research, as it offers millions of articles about it. Read through real estate journals, estate blogs, and other online resources.

3. Get a mentor
Sometimes a mentor can decide your whole journey in syndication. A mentor may be the difference between the success of your syndicate program and its failure. The input of an experienced syndicate will help you to find your way around the whole syndication process. Remember, the mentor has passed through this stage you are currently in. He or she understands the pros and cons of the business. Their mentorship may

assist you to avoid the potential pitfalls of those who have failed in implementing the idea. If getting the right mentor proves difficult for you, check out these tested and proven tips:

- Establish a friendly relationship with an experienced syndicator: There are thousands of people who use syndication to improve their investments and income. Look for such people and learn from them. Otherwise, you can consult online directories and get a list of real estate investors who might live right in your neighborhood.

- Have experienced members on your team. By watching them from close quarters, you will understand how they work and follow suit.

4. Follow the blueprint

Follow the steps of others before you. As you learn from your mentor, look at others who have made a success of the same principle. Learn what they did right and mimic that while being mindful to avoid their mistakes. This will make it easier for you.

Of course, syndication has a special blueprint that gives potential syndicates the guidelines to make a success out of it. The blueprint has been used by many real estate investors for years to launch their syndicate careers. I have included it in the back of the book as a bonus chapter from which I hope you can gain great insight with which to form your own syndication plan.

A Syndicator's Five Spinning Plates

You may recall an image earlier in the book...did it look like me?!

When I think of all of the responsibilities of a syndicator, I always think of those entertainers who can manage lots of moving parts at one time.

For some, it might be the jugglers at the circus who can keep all those bowling pins up in the air without ever dropping a single one. For others, it might be the Harlem Globetrotter who can spin basketballs on his fingers, his toes, his nose, and his head - all at the same time.

For me, it is the plate spinners, the street entertainers that I used to watch growing up in New Delhi, India. I was mesmerized at how they could place those plates on the end of sticks and start them spinning. They would start with one or two and keep adding more and more. I thought it must take incredible focus, not to mention flexibility, balance, and commitment. It would be tough not to concentrate on the toughest plate to keep spinning, but a good plate spinner could not have tunnel vision; he had to give equal time and attention to each of the spinning plates

That idea stuck with me into adulthood and into my real estate career. One day, when I was working on a deal, contacting brokers, negotiating a contract with help of my attorney, getting the paperwork together for the lenders, taking calls from investors and interviewing property managers, it suddenly hit me - I was a PLATE SPINNER!

Talent aside, that's what we do when we operate as the syndicator in a multifamily, multiple investor real estate deal. We must be focused, busy, and diligent as we keep all of the parts moving. Daily, a good syndicator is building **strong teams**, compiling **investor lists** and **cultivating relationships** with those investors, working on getting the **underwriting** for your deal, **qualifying** for your loan, and planning for your **property takeover and management**. See what I mean? Those five plates must be spinning all the time, and you will find that each one takes a fairly good amount of time, energy, and attention.

Syndication Principles and Strategies

I want to stress here that the principles, blueprints, strategies, and knowledge that I will share in the following chapters can be used for any kind of syndication. Once you have a strong business plan to RAISE CAPITAL from interested investors; you can build a new hotel, buy a warehouse, do many renovations simultaneously of single family homes, buy apartments or multifamily, buy office buildings, senior communities or shopping centers. The world is wide open to undertake big projects just because you control now **millions of dollars through syndication!**

However, I want to also mention that instead of doing any or all of the above commercial and retail investments. The world of purchasing apartments complexes also called multifamily (duplex, triplex, fourplex or 50 units or 100 units or 500 units) really got me excited due to a whole lot of reasons.

In the next chapter, I want to tell you all the reasons why I made that BEST decision to dig deeper into acquiring apartments (multifamily). Why I got so passionate about learning the art of syndication and raising lots of money to scale up faster. To be truthful, our single-family home rentals scattered all over many states were not bringing in the cash flows we were expecting.

With full conviction, I can tell you that I am even more passionate after 14 years since I made that decision to enter this great asset class of the commercial real estate. I did not leave any stone unturned to learn and practice everything I could to purchase apartments by forming great teams. Actually in the crash of 2007-08, **multifamily was the only sector** that weathered the storm better than any other sector of RE.

I am so glad that I chose this sector of the commercial real estate. You will get hooked also, I am sure, and you will also taste your first success or even tenth if you are in it already!! Without learning and practicing syndication, my world would have turned out very differently, hence the reason for writing this book and spreading the word through my mastermind enthusiastic coaching sessions.

After the next chapter on *Why Multifamily?*, I will break down these plates. Wait! I didn't mean breaking plates - that's what we don't want to do. We will be examining each plate that a syndicator spins, learning what we can about each aspect of being that plate spinning syndicator.

CHAPTER TWO

Why Multifamily?

As its name states, multifamily property covers different types of residential real estate with the exception of single-family buildings. For the purposes of this book and teaching you to syndicate real estate investments, we will not address single-family units, specifically rental houses. Instead, let's focus our attention on multifamily properties and why they can provide the best bang for your buck. Since terms can sometimes vary by region (although that doesn't apply so much to real estate), let's begin with some basic examples of a multifamily property.

The most common buildings within this subgroup are:

- Apartments
- Townhomes
- Co-ops, and so on

Real Estate

The rental property in real estate can be divided into two main categories: single-family and multifamily. The latter is our focus.

Single-family properties have a single unit available for rent.

Multifamily properties have more than one rental space. It is also called an apartment complex.

Even among apartments, there are a variety of property types. The chart below will give you a quick look at the varieties.

1. **High-rise**: These buildings consist of nine or more floors, and the tenants within a high-rise are served by at least one elevator.

2. **Mid-rise**: A mid-rise apartment is typically a multi-story building that is located on the outskirts of an urban area. A mid-rise will typically have only one elevator.

3. **Garden-style**: This is an apartment that is built in the form of a garden. Garden-style apartments are usually found in urban or suburban locations and may contain as many as three stories.

4. **Walk-up**: A walk-up apartment building will have between four and six stories without an elevator.

5. **Manufactured housing community**: Manufactured homes are built on grounds that are leased by the community.

6. **Special-purpose housing**: As the name implies, special-purpose housing is multifamily apartments that are built to meet the specific needs of a particular population within the community. For instance, it may be hostel accommodations for students or a home for senior citizens. Special-purpose housing also includes subsidized housing such as low-income housing or special need housing.

Why Multifamily Real Estate?

Countless individuals dabble in real estate with a handful of rental houses and maybe a duplex or two, and some enjoy a comfortable living from their small investment. But since our plan is financial independence, we need to look at a bigger market and a better return. The multifamily market has carved a niche for itself in the commercial real estate sector. No matter the condition of the economy, the multifamily market has a track record of performing better than all other classes of real estate. This sector of real estate has given investors unique high returns and lower risks compared with other sectors. This has made the multi-family investment the most advantageous, stable, and safest market in which to invest within the real estate world.

Going back on memory lane with Vinney

When I started my real estate investing career about 35 years back, I thought buying single-family homes to rent was a great investment and would potentially secure my future wealth. So, I began buying these homes and learning the business that went with it, such as financing, upkeep, and the challenges that went along with owning these rental homes. Since we (my team and I) bought properties in states scattered across the country, we chose to hire property management companies to manage them. The tax benefits of owning and renting them were good, but the cash flows were erratic. However, we just kept on purchasing and holding onto them while looking forward to their payoff in our retirement.

But I must confess that we sold all of them in 2017—with one exception - a duplex that yields a very nice monthly cash-flow even after 8 years after we acquired it.

Single-family and multifamily homes are great for both seasoned investors and up-and-coming investors. As with any real estate deal, please do your due diligence to ensure the deal makes sense financially and fits your personal goals for your investing business.

Scattered Houses vs. Units All on One Site

Obviously, the capital required for unexpected issues tends to eat into your cash flow very quickly. These expenses can include—but are not limited to—the purchase of a new boiler, replacement of or maintenance of an air-conditioning system, garage malfunctions, tree roots getting too close to the structure - and the list goes on.

Some people really do prefer single-family units for real estate investment. So, in fairness, a comparison of the advantages of both is offered below.

Three Advantages of Single-Family Rental Properties

1. Single-family units are easier to get into and require a single, smaller loan or cash deal.

2. Appreciation is tied directly to neighborhood growth.

3. These units are easier to sell when the times comes to do so.

Three Advantages of Multifamily Rental Properties

1. **Multifamily properties generate higher cash flows**, which tends to be more consistent due to less effect of vacancy. For example, if you have twenty units, and two tenants leave, your property is still 90% occupied. Bigger pool of tenants-less risk!

2. **Multifamily property owners have more control over value.** The value is based on the net income generated by the multifamily property. By adding value, the rents can be increased over time as the leases expire.

3. **Economies of scale.** This is a big one! In the case of a needed roof replacement, consider the fact that, with twenty units, you still only need to replace two or three roofs (one per building).

If, however, you are dealing with single-family homes, you may have twenty separate roofs in need of replacement within just a short span of time. Quite simply, maintenance requests can be handled much more efficiently in one location than when your units are scattered across an entire city or region.

Actually, there are a lot more than just three advantages to investing in multifamily real estate. For me, after looking at so many ways to invest in the market, I decided to choose only one path: multifamily investing. I, wholeheartedly, encourage you and other investors to choose this route, also. It made sense 14 years back, and it still holds true today. It just makes all the sense in the world!

Even MORE Advantages of Multifamily Investing

4. **Scalability is much easier in multifamily.** Rather than purchasing individual properties and slowly growing your business one transaction at a time, in multifamily you are purchasing 20 units or 100 units in one transaction.

5. **Forcing appreciation in multifamily properties is easier compared to single-family housing.** When you give your apartment building (or even a four-plex or eight-plex) more curb appeal, you will push up the value of the property exponentially. Think about it – if you fix things in the property that make it more appealing as a living space for tenants by adding a nice media center, a dog park, or a friendlier laundry room space (all of which can be done in larger multifamily complexes, too), you will attract tenants to your building versus another landlord's building. That's what you want! And, because your tenants will want to stay, you are simultaneously creating bigger and steadier cash flow.

6. **More income in multifamily assets.** We call these *bill-back* utilities (RUBS). The residents are billed for a portion of the

water, trash, sewer, and pest control services out of the total master bill that the owner receives. Along with paying the monthly rent, residents pay a flat fee or a proportional amount each month for these services. Most of the multifamily properties are individually metered for electricity, and each resident pays that separately.

7. **Great tax breaks come with investing in multifamily properties**. When you provide housing it really is a good thing. The government thinks so, too. The city in which the property is located likes the idea because you are helping the residents of that city by providing clean, safe, affordable housing to people who might not otherwise find it. As a result, you can gain all sorts of tax incentives (also known as tax breaks).

8. **Multifamily properties hold their value.** Once the property is rehabbed and you have made it attractive to tenants, it will also attract other investors who will be interested in buying the property later (if you ever want to sell). You will have put in place everything required to attract and retain tenants. That means steady cash flow, which is mighty appealing to investors.

9. **Investing in multifamily housing allows you to change lives.** We take pride in providing great places for the residents to live. We provide jobs to staff members at the property, as well as the vendors who service your property. Most importantly, though, through syndications, we help a lot of investors who are doing well in their profession but don't have the time for hands-on work with their multifamily properties.

Trends bode well for this strategy!

Are you convinced? Well, if you need any other incentives or assurances that multifamily investments are the avenue to take on your journey to financial independence, consider these trends:

- 75 million Baby Boomers are headed into retirement.

- Many of today's apartment complexes may be converted to retirement communities in the future; the Baby Boomers are also downsizing.

- Most millennials are not buying homes.

- It is becoming more expensive to build new apartment buildings.

To answer the question, *"Why multifamily real estate even further?"* allow me to share the following reasons:

The market is resilient!
In moments of economic recession, the multifamily housing market has proven to be the most resilient, maintaining its high reputation and resisting the effects of an ailing economy. This stability gives the investors the assurance that their money is safe.

It has great demand!
The demand for multifamily properties has skyrocketed over the past few years. This is not unrelated to the values of these properties in comparison with other properties in the sector. Due to many factors, the growth of people renting is growing rapidly.

It carries a lower vacancy risk!
When compared with other real estate properties like offices and rental houses, the vacancy risks of multifamily real estate are significantly lower.

It demonstrates a high growth rate!

Benefiting from the population growth of an area, multifamily housing does not rely much on business cycles for existence. People will always need a place to live!

Property management is more efficient!

It is much easier to manage a multifamily property than it is to manage single properties. For instance, maintaining twelve units within one property will be less challenging and less expensive to maintain that twelve single properties in different locations.

If the properties are scattered all around town or even in different states, you could possibly need three or four different management companies to maintain them.

Consider, though, that one multifamily property single location, even with twelve units, can easily be managed by one part-time property manager. Even if you have a 50-unit apartment, the maintenance job will be handled by one manager or a single management company. The company will oversee the collection of rent, tenant issues, and building maintenance, among other issues.

Forced appreciation is easier!

I will talk in more detail later about this industry term and about how to use the concept of Forced Appreciation to raise the value of a property with the objective of increasing the income generated by that property. This, too, can be much more easily accomplished with a multifamily property than with single-family units. For now, just think about the fact that whatever facelift you do on a single-family property will impact that home only and in doing so will have a very limited effect in comparison to enhancements made on a multifamily property. The financial reward for you in improving a single-family property is greatly diminished in comparison.

Taxes

As mentioned above, owning apartments is a tremendous tax benefit. As in any business, we are able to deduct all the expenses incurred in administering the management of the apartment, and the benefit of deducting the depreciation often results in losses at the bottom line. This happens even when there is a large net income generated during the years of performance. This is a huge benefit that is not realized in other means of investing. We use the LLC owning the assets as a pass-through entity for Taxes. This way the whole effect of depreciation, profit, or losses are passed through to the Class A investor members and to us the Class B members.

Tax breaks are available

Providing housing for people is considered a good gesture by many people. The government shares that sentiment! You are rendering a good service to people by helping them to have access to safe, clean, and affordable housing that, otherwise, might not be available. As such, you may benefit from a variety of different tax incentives or tax breaks from the government, possibly even providing you with grants to offset all the upfront costs on the property. In some situations, you may end up not paying any property taxes at all.

Depreciation

Depreciation is one great benefit of owning real estate. Simply put, depreciation can allow you to reduce the amount of taxes you pay due to accounting standards. It is treated as a paper loss. Even though the asset is producing cash flow due to the collection of rents, minus expenses, and mortgage, we are able to depreciate the structures (usually 70%-80% of the value of the apartment buildings) over 27.5 years, straight line. There are other avenues where we can deduct larger depreciation amounts through "cost segregation" also called "**accelerated depreciation**" in the first 5 to 15 years, thus yielding more tax benefits.

They hold their value!

The first thing to do after purchasing a multifamily property is to renovate it according to the latest property trends. Even some minimal renovation to the property will increase its value and make it appealing to other investors should you ever decide to sell the property. You have also increased the property's value to its current tenants, those who may not yet be ready to leave the property, and that guarantees continued cash flow, which is an added bonus for you, the new owner.

Unless you are planning on being a slumlord (in which case you should put down this book now), proper maintenance of the property should be of utmost importance to you. The floor, the roof, and the environment around the units must be put in good shape, and those occasional repairs should be carried out swiftly and happily.

You are changing lives!

Providing housing is a great investment in humankind! When you invest in multifamily properties you are having a positive influence on many people:

1. Residents in your community
2. Teams of people managing them
3. Vendors servicing your communities
4. Investors receiving cash flows and equity gains
5. Neighborhood businesses and facilities

Multifamily Properties are easier to finance!

While many people believe that it will be easier to get a loan for a single-family home than a multi-family home, those people are mistaken. In fact, that notion is far from the truth. In reality, it is easier to get a loan for a multifamily property than for a single dwelling. Although it takes more money to finance a multifamily property, lenders are willing to take the risk because multifamily properties guarantee steady cash flow, something that single-family units cannot do so easily.

For instance, if the tenant of a single-family property leaves, the home becomes 100% vacant which is bad for business. However, if a tenant of a 10-unit, multifamily property leaves the property, the vacancy is 10%, leaving 90% of the property as a source of income until the vacant apartment is rented again. This ensures steady cash flow for the property owner and reduces the probability of a foreclosure, a valid reason for lenders to be willing to give the borrower a loan. It really is a less-risky investment for the bank and for you in comparison to ownership of a single-family rental property.

Debt leverage

It is only in real estate that the banks, financial institutions, insurance companies, Fannie Mae, and Freddie Mac are willing to partner with you in such an advantageous way, providing loans from 65% to as high as 80% of the value of the real estate you are purchasing. You have to only put down 35% to as low as 20% to control the investment.

Consider stocks, bonds, precious metals, and even cryptocurrency — Lenders typically do not provide loans to purchase any of these. Real estate, then, is an excellent vehicle of wealth building due to "debt leverage." It's important to understand that this leverage can go the other way as well, and that's why we talk about having a safety net through your Debt-Coverage ratio later on in the book.

Building a portfolio is easy!

If an investor wants to quickly build a portfolio of rental units, the best way to go about it is to invest in multifamily properties. This is a much more enticing prospect than the idea of buying twenty different units, which will require the appraisal and inspection of twenty different properties in just as many locations. On top of that, there is the potential of having to hire twenty different managers, and you might even have to take out twenty different loans. Whew! That's a headache!! It is much easier and less time-consuming to buy one twenty-unit multifamily property and avoid the extra time, hassle, and stress.

Debt pay-down

As rental and other incomes are collected monthly in apartments, the mortgage (interest on loan and the principal) is paid out monthly. Consequently, the loan balance amount, which is your principal, is decreased monthly. If we keep the asset over 30 years and pay down the debt for that long, we will own the apartment complex free and clear. Mind you, it all got paid for by the rents collected with no money out of pocket.

Appreciating rental rates in the future

- This is another great benefit. As the market improves where the apartment is located, a 2%-4% growth rate in rent is usually expected. In certain hot markets, the rent appreciations can even go as high as 7%-9% for a few years. But it is prudent to take a conservative approach and keep this appreciation to a lower percentage.

- **It affords you the opportunity to hire a property management company!** Sometimes, due to one reason or the other, hiring a management company is the ideal choice to make. These management companies have the responsibility of screening tenants, collecting house rent, maintaining the building (and, in some cases, the grounds), along with other responsibilities. Hiring them takes a whole lot of the burden off the shoulders of investors who can afford their fees. Often, an investor in single family unit homes may find that the fees associated with a property management company prohibit using one, even if they feel that is the best thing for them to do. This is not the same with an investor in a big multifamily property. The monthly income from the property gives the owner/investor the financial power to hire a company that takes care of his investment, allowing them to channel their efforts and time towards other important things.

Many real estate investors go into multifamily due to the many benefits mentioned above. If you are interested in making a living from real estate investment and want steady cash flow, investing in multifamily property really is one of the best options for you. You will contribute immensely to society, add value to people's lives, and be assured of passive income for as long as you are in business.

Property Classification

As I attempt to sell you on this idea of multifamily real estate, perhaps some classification of the various property types would prove useful. Property classification: What does that even mean? This is another common question I receive from new investors. We classified real estate properties into three categories: Class A, Class B, and Class C. Let's break each category down and, in doing so, see why these classifications matter.

What and Why?

Property classification is a simple way of differentiating one type of property from another. It is developed and used by lenders, investors, and brokers to discuss the rating and quality of a piece of real estate. This classification method makes it easier to communicate quickly and efficiently amongst the various stakeholders in the deal about the quality and rating of a property. For investors, property class is an important factor to consider because each class represents a different level of risk and return. The following criteria are used in this classification method.

Criteria of property classification

- Income of tenant
- Age of property
- Location of property
- Amenities
- Appreciation and rental income
- Growth prospect

The combination of these factors will determine which letter grade will be assigned to a property. Here are the various classifications:

Class A

As its name implies, this category represents the premium quality properties in the area. A common trend among them is their age; they are usually built within the last 15 years, which makes them relatively new in comparison to the buildings in other classes.

This category is generally marked by...

- Best amenities
- Low vacancy rates
- Tenants whose incomes are higher

The location of these properties is another criterion that distinguishes them as Class A. They are usually in prime locations in the market. This makes the demand high and increases the potential rental income they will generate. This is not a problem considering the type of tenants that opt for Class A buildings. These properties typically have few maintenance issues, as they are (almost) always professionally managed.

Class B

The quality and the price of the properties in this subcategory is a little bit lower. These properties are usually older than the properties in Class A and are occupied by lower income tenants. While the location may not be on par with that of Class A, the location is still very good and has more value than the buildings in the next, lower Class C. The rental income per unit is less than that of Class A largely due to the location. Owners can expect to have a few more maintenance issues because the buildings are older than Class A properties.

Most of the buildings in this group are well-maintained and are still popular with investors because, with just a little tweaking here and there, they may be upgraded to Class B+ or Class A. This makes the Class B buildings a good investment for some investors who might not have the financial power to invest in Class A property. Class B can also be resilient during economic downturns, as Class A tenants may transition to Class B apartments if their financial situation forces them to do so.

Class C

The properties in this subcategory are the oldest in our market. They are typically more than 20 years old, and they are sometimes located in less-than-desirable locations. Class C properties usually need renovation. Because of this, Class C buildings tend to have the lowest rental rates in a market.

Each subcategory carries its own set of pros and cons. Why are Class A properties the preferred first choice of investors? Because those investors feel more confident in investing their money in properties that do not require much additional cost to improve. The fact that these buildings are new and require no renovation removes the burden of extra expenditure upfront. Despite their favorable attributes, though, running a Class A property can be challenging during an economic crisis when high-income earners may be faced with lower income or temporary unemployment as a result of a loss of job or layoff. Class A properties will typically have lower returns when you first acquire them because of this risk-reward tradeoff.

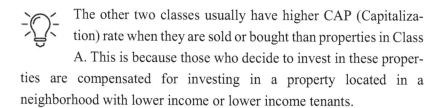 The other two classes usually have higher CAP (Capitalization) rate when they are sold or bought than properties in Class A. This is because those who decide to invest in these properties are compensated for investing in a property located in a neighborhood with lower income or lower income tenants.

If you need a property with capital preservation, go for Class A properties. Classes B and C properties are ideal for you if you are looking at capital appreciation.

Before we move on from why multifamily properties are the way to go, let me provide you with a few more reasons why I recommend this type of investment. The following seven steps to building wealth through apartment investing are sure to entice you further.

I sincerely hope that you are seeing the major advantages in apartment investing, often called multifamily investing. With Millennials liking portability and the downsizing of the Baby Boomers population, the demand for apartment rentals is predicted to be strong and increasingly sustained well into the future.

As you can see, I really am very bullish on investing in multifamily real estate, as opposed to single-family or other commercial sectors. I sincerely hope that this chapter will cause you to investigate diversifying and beginning your investment in multifamily real estate. Syndication is the best game - pooling money together in accordance with the SEC (U.S. Securities and Exchange Commission) rules and regulations to leverage the greatest turn-around on your investment as we discussed in the previous chapter. Now let share with you the five plates I have been talking about in great detail in the next few chapters.

CHAPTER THREE

Plate #1 – Building Great Teams

Individuals score points, but TEAMS win games."
– Zig Ziglar

Building Your Real Estate Dream Investment Teams

Whether you realized it before now or not, real estate investing takes a team. It is not a solo sport. It doesn't matter if you are doing one deal or twenty. You must build a team to be successful. I suppose there is a real estate company or two in every town in America who has that one broker and listing agent that call themselves the DREAM TEAM. They do that for good reason - teams just make it more fun and more profitable. The same principle applies to multifamily real estate and syndications.

Finding an emerging market, building relationships with real estate brokers, making the purchase, and managing an investment property takes many different professionals. These individuals are all part of your investment team. Finding great people to work with will make your life easier. Having a quality, well-skilled team is essential to your real estate investing success. Knowing where to go when questions arise will make your life easier and will enable you to make more money. So, let's spend some time talking about how you can build your dream team.

Along the way, your team will help you avoid costly mistakes. When you invest in real estate, there are many questions that must be answered. Questions such as: Where will I find opportunities? How will I get them financed? What needs to be included in the contract? Along with those questions come many feelings of uncertainty and insecurity. Should I take this step? What if I'm making a mistake? This is too hard and depressing!

The good news is that you don't have to go at it alone any more than you have to have all the answers. It is not nearly as important to know all the answers as it is to know where to find those answers. First among your most valuable resources is a quality team that will help you answer those questions. They will even help you answer the questions you didn't even know to ask. With the right team, you are sure to be more successful and avoid mistakes.

Surround Yourself with Passionate People

Before delving into the makeup of these teams, it is, once again, a good time to talk about attitude. You want to make sure that your team consists of people who share your passion for your deal. Happiness breeds creative thinking, and when you worry about the little details, it causes you to be unhappy and unable to think as clearly as when everything is in order. Setting and reaching your professional goals is essential for personal happiness and professional success, but you should know that you cannot make it on your own. Bringing people into your investment strategy that are just as excited as you are will birth the type of daily happiness and long-term success you desire as you start pushing toward reaching your goals.

PLATE #1 – BUILDING GREAT TEAMS · 55

The Teams

The vital members of your teams will be brokers, contractors, due diligence experts, legal counsel (real estate and syndication), and management companies.

The Six Essential Teams for Any Real Estate Investor

There are six key teams you need to have in place if you are to be successful in real estate investment. They are...

1. Multifamily Underwriting and Acquisition Team

The first group of professionals you need to have is an acquisition team. This team consists of the people who help you locate and identify potential opportunities. Without opportunities flowing your way, you cannot make it as a real estate investor. This group will be made up of Real Estate and Loan brokers, bank officers, inspectors, and appraisers, all who will help you find quality opportunities and maximize the value of the property when you decide to sell.

2. Legal Team

The next team you are going to need is a legal team. Quality legal work is extremely important when purchasing and owning real estate. Attorneys can help protect you as you buy, own, and sell real estate. They can handle contracts, set up the appropriate legal structure, prepare the closing documents, and make sure you have legal leases. The attorneys you use in a transaction can consist of real estate, transaction, or contract attorneys. You may also want securities and exchange attorneys on your team if you are going to be raising money from outside investors.

3. Equity Investors

Equity (Down Payment) is the money needed to buy a property. If you are financing a portion of your purchase, equity is the amount you need outside of the financing. This can come from an individual or from a group of investors (syndication). If you use a group, you need to make sure you follow rules for pooling investors' monies. The Securities and Exchange Commission has very strict guidelines that must be followed precisely when syndicating with investors. You can check with your local, state, and federal authorities to find out the specifics in your area, and a qualified securities and exchange attorney can also be very helpful knowledgeable about these guidelines.

4. Financing Team

If you do not plan on paying all cash for your next investment, you will need to have others to help obtain the needed financing. This team consists of lending institutions, private individuals, and mortgage brokers. These are individuals or institutions that will provide a significant portion of the money needed to purchase your next investment property. Personally, I have really found in my last 26 syndications that having great loan brokers on the team puts you at a tremendous advantage in the process. They have this incredible ability to write a tremendous story and bio of you and your experiences that, when presented to the lending institutions, Fannie Mae, or Freddie Mac, goes a long way in convincing them to accept the risk and loan the money.

5. Property Management Team

Once you have purchased an investment property, one of the most critical teams is your property management group. This team sees to the daily operation of your property. These individuals or groups will take care of repairs and maintenance, collect the rent, and handle the leasing of your units. In our experience, this is the team that can make or break your investment. (NOTE: Because of the importance of this team, after our third acquisition, we formed our own property management company by hiring the top Multifamily Property Consulting Group in the United States. They took care of making sure we were professional in our adherence to the Fair Housing Laws and the proper methods of recruiting and renting, as well as using the best accounting software for our type of operation,).

PLATE #1 – BUILDING GREAT TEAMS · 57

The management companies are well informed on the trends in the market. They can tell you about:

- Emerging market pockets
- Market trends
- Rent trends
- Potential sellers
- Vacancy rates & collections

If rather than managing the property yourself, you plan on using a third-party property management company, it is essential to choose a company that is experienced in the area, type, and size of your property. A commercial property management company is a great organization to have on your team. You can seek their professional input on what part of the town is nice or not. Additionally, they can provide you with the most current information on the collections, a five-year analysis of the property and a ten-year projection for it going forward. You can rely on them to be versed in the emerging market, the amount of value added, and the potential of new value to be added.

While the broker should be providing you with much of that information, you should consider a company like this to help with both the acquisition portion and the management part of the deal. For that reason, we recommend hiring an outside management company with a proven success rate and profitable track record. You will want plenty of references from them of individual real estate investors or groups that are their clients. Likewise, you will want to familiarize yourself with their organization, their bookkeeping system and software, and the reports they provide to their customers. When you partner with the right property management company, owning multifamily housing can be much more enjoyable.

6. Accounting Team

Here is where a lot of investors tend to skimp, but that is a big mistake. This team is what we call the heart of the operation. All the rental collections, income streams, and property management expenses run through this department. This team is responsible for seeing to it that all funds received are deposited into the operational checking accounts of the multifamily syndication.

We typically set up three individual accounts per property: (1) Operating Expenses; (2) Investors' Account; and (3) Escrow Account. Having accurate and up-to-date accounting is essential to operating your real estate investment business and ensuring cash flow for your investors. Even if you hire outside management, you need to know what is happening financially on your property. Don't ever be a silent partner when it comes to the accounting for your investment. *How else will you accurately determine if you are making money?* An investment property with poor records is an investment property with real problems. And, as a side note, be very wary of buying properties from anyone who cannot provide accurate and up-to-date financials.

Team Members

Some suggested individuals to invite to be part of your team.

1. Commercial broker(s)
2. Real estate attorney(s)
3. Loan broker(s)
4. General contractor(s) and/or due diligence inspector
5. Appraiser
6. Commercial property management company

Your TEAM members must be local to your investment market. They will act as your eyes and ears.

I have found that if I do not live in the area in which I am investing, I need to build a team from among that market. It helps ensure that you have first-hand knowledge of the area. Often the "locals" can provide much-needed information that will assist in marketing and occupying

PLATE #1 – BUILDING GREAT TEAMS · 59

your multifamily property. They know the property's reputation, its potential, and, in many cases, the tenants who will occupy the units.

Learn to Diversify

No one person can do it all. Real estate agents cannot list a house, perform repairs, inspect it, and secure financing for a potential buyer. Every person along the chain has a specific purpose. Your motivation may blind you to the fact that there are not enough hours in your day to accomplish everything you want to do. When you learn to diversify, share the load among a fully-equipped team, you empower others to really function as team players. Remember, you are not giving up control, but you are, instead, trusting others to do what you know you could do. And guess what? They might even do it better than you!

Some Very Important Team Members: The Brokers

As a syndicator who is putting together a deal, there are some key players that you may want to consider for your team. You will, as you continue in the business, need to be building a strong team of commercial brokers. So, it is a good idea to think about including them on the inside of the deal. They are good people to bond with, so talk with them on a regular basis. Send cards and gifts from time to time and work to rise to their top-level list of investors. Concentrate on the *Listing Agents*, or what we call the Sellers' Brokers. Buyers' Brokers are beneficial to you as you look to purchase, but they are not the ones who will help you make money down the road. Listing agents/sellers' brokers can be valuable assets. Once they get to know you, you will find that they may even seek you out to bring the listing to you. As with any business, there are the "inside deals." We call them these the **pocket listings**.

Pocket listings are the "put-it-away for a few days or weeks" listings. These are the ones they haven't even told anyone about yet. Even pre-pocket listings, those on which the ink is not yet dried, are even better listings. Those are the ones we keep asking these agents and brokers about in our ongoing conversations with them. You know what I'm talk-ing about...over coffee or a round of golf, asking them questions like "Hey, do you know any owners that are thinking of selling in this par-ticular market?" When you have a strong relationship with these brokers, you can typically grab a deal before it even becomes public knowledge.

As you are building those broker relationships, you can frequent the websites that list multifamily properties for sale in your area. Check out *www.loopnet.com* and *www.costar.com*. These are good resources when you are looking to purchase, but keep in mind that the listings on there are out there for the whole world to see and have already gone through about five layers.

The Listing Path

1. Napkin Listing - only fortunate inner circle investors get these

2. Pre-pocket – only a few investors are exposed to the deal

3. Pocket – a few 'A' list clients get access to the deal

4. Office – the brokers share the listing with a few colleagues and friends

5. Office Floor – the listing gets shared with the entire company and other large branches

6. Popular websites – the listing reaches the entire public

Let's briefly detail each of these six pre-public layers.

Napkin Listing: I invented this term as I saw brokers giving me the address of the properties right from the coffee table as they wrote out the information from the seller on a napkin while having coffee, lunch or dinner. It was also observed that I would get the same address and info for the same property from a few brokers after they met with the

PLATE #1 – BUILDING GREAT TEAMS · 61

sellers, the following day or after a couple of days. Actually, no broker had the written signed off-listing; they were all trying to get that precious listing!! I always stayed true to the FIRST broker who gave that lead to deal with.

Pre-pocket: The brokers alone know about this one. They are mulling over in their heads who to let know about the upcoming investment opportunity. The property may not even be listed yet, but the brokers know it is about to be. Like everyone, they want to make as much money as possible with the least effort, so they can share these deals with those they know would be in the market for a quick closing on a nice property.

Pocket: The property is being listed, and the broker is preparing to make it public. However, there are still some days or maybe even a week or two between their preparation and the public listing. They will willingly share this deal with a select group of investors. You are cultivating these broker relationships so that you will be part of that select group.

Office: For whatever reason, no one has jumped on the investment property during the pre-pocket or pocket phase. No need to worry; maybe another investor just is not in a situation where he or she can jump on it. So, the broker will make it known to a few close colleagues and friends. Again, this is a group to which you want to belong.

Office Floor: When it gets placed on the office floor, anyone in the company can take advantage of the opportunity. Depending on the size of the company, multiple branches of operation may even become knowledgeable about the property, and they probably have their lists of investors (like your broker does) with whom they will immediately share it. The listing is becoming closer and closer to the public "grab bag" phase.

Web Listing: Now it is out there for the world to see. Maybe as a single-family unit investor, you are familiar with websites like *Zillow* and

Trulia. On the multifamily and commercial side, there are others like the ones mentioned, *LoopNet* and *Costar.* Both are good sites, but anyone and everyone looking for multifamily investment property is now able to find out everything about the listings. You are now in the fight for the property if you want it, and you will wish you had known about it earlier...maybe in the pre-pocket phase.

What to do prior to analyzing a deal

1. Always look to establish relationships with potential investors.
2. Find the emerging markets in the area you would like to invest
3. Surround yourself with professionals in the real estate arena.
    - Brokers
    - Lenders
    - Mortgage brokers
    - Local banks
    - Appraisers
    - Property inspectors

Developing an effective team in your organization can seem like a simple and straightforward task, however, it can be difficult to execute and put into practice. Members of your organization want to be able to believe in the process and realize the wonderful outcomes that come from working together as opposed to individually. So, it is up to the manager to ensure that enthusiasm is garnered and nourished. Mind mapping and vision boarding are super techniques.

The most important building block to develop an effective team is communication, so it is imperative to develop the necessary skills to communicate effectively with each other.

To keep the teamwork fire burning, you need to establish regular and open lines of communication and monitor how the group interacts. Learning to communicate effectively is not a simple one-step process

PLATE #1 – BUILDING GREAT TEAMS · 63

and requires work from all sides. It is a great idea to have weekly meetings in which the manager is present in order to see how the team interacts with each other and offer feedback on their achievements and to constructively evaluate how well your team accomplishes their goals together.

Here are some of the characteristics of a highly effective team, according to scientific research.

1. Emotional intelligence of each team member
2. A good mix of introverts and extroverts
3. They share the same stories
4. They make time for humor
5. They communicate proactively
6. Great leadership

An effective team is one that has cohesion. To accomplish this your team members, need to exhibit the following skills:

Openness – Team members need to be willing to get to know each other and open up about themselves. In doing so, they will realize that they all have diverse backgrounds and interests. This helps them to be more open to new ideas and differing viewpoints.

Trust – Team members need to trust each other enough to be comfortable with sharing ideas and feelings. As this trust builds, team members learn to be honest and respectful in their approach to each other.

Respect – It is important for the team not to focus on who to blame when something goes wrong. Instead, the team needs to work out how to fix it and how to learn from the mistake. Constructive feedback and mutual respect, rather than blame, will help a team achieve results much faster.

The following six keys to an effective and successful team have been proven to enable teams to achieve high-performance status as quickly as possible.

Effective and successful teams always:

1. Establish clearly defined team goals.
2. Develop a plan of action.
3. Identify roles and responsibilities.
4. Measure and monitor progress.
5. Ensure all team members are engaged and committed.
6. Work together with commitment and determination.

I cannot overemphasize the importance of good teams. I can tell you from experience that this business is much more profitable and much more fun when you are surrounded by like-minded people who all have the same end goal - investing for a better future. These teams will be your lifeline. You are already going to be spinning five plates as a syndicator. Without a great team in place, you will find yourself spinning even more, and that is very difficult to do and very draining for you and for your family. So, start making your list now of your DREAM TEAM!

CHAPTER FOUR

Plate #2 – Building Lists and Relationships: All About the Investors

Allow me to let you in on a little secret. Now, don't let this hurt your feelings, but not every investor will want to be a part of your deal! Just as each person in the world is unique, everybody - husband, wife, relative, friend - has his or her own individual level of risk tolerance and experience. Perhaps, from previous investments, they have incurred losses. Maybe on another deal, they made money.

There is no way to know what motivates a potential investor's overall attitude or determines the kinds of risks he or she will take? What is important to remember is that the investor is simply declining to take a risk on the deal. Ultimately, he or she is not really rejecting you. Remember, this isn't personal; it's business! As such, it may be that the investor is not in a position to invest right now. Or perhaps, he or she is not yet sold on the benefits and the returns. Maybe he or she is not confident in the projections the investment is showing for the next three to five, or three to seven years.

For those whose answer is no, just smile, thank them for their time, and part company in such a friendly way that the door will remain open the next time. *No* may not mean *No;* it might just mean ***not yet.***

If you have already heard no, I would say *congratulations!* That means you are off to a running start. You have started determining who your potential investors might be. So, what if the first one or two...or five said no. Let's focus on the ones who remain candidates for partners in your deal.

Your Circles of Influence

I would say suggest that you start an Excel worksheet on which you write down your **circles of influence.** That means that you go ahead and look at all the people you know, beginning with relatives.

First Circle of Influence
It makes sense that your first circle of influence, those closest to you would be your relatives. The circles then expand to friends, business acquaintances, and beyond. I must confess that, in my case, when I started out, I was not convinced of how successful I would be, so I did not want to involve my relatives, but you can!

Second Circle of Influence
From there, take a look at your close friends, the ones you have known for five, ten, maybe fifteen years - friends who believe in you, who know what you are doing and might like to know about multi-family investing.

Third Circle of Influence
Then, consider those you might know from your church or civic organization. There are some very accomplished people at church and in the local civic groups. That would be your third circle of influence.

Fourth Circle of Influence
That takes us to the fourth one, which will be your client base. If you are, like I am, a real estate broker, it is easy to go back and look at a big database you have already compiled. It is a wonderful list of potential investors compiled of the people you have sold homes to - people with whom you have already built a relationship. You never know how much

PLATE #2 – BUILDING LISTS AND RELATIONSHIPS · 67

money they might have in their retirement accounts, in their cash positions or in their bank account, earning 1% or 2%, at best. And you are offering a chance for them to invest at a preferred rate of 8%. At 8%, you just quadrupled their returns! On top of that 8%, they are also *equity investors*, meaning you are bringing them in as "Class A" members to the syndication. They are not on the loan; they are passively investing in your deal, enjoying quarterly returns. However, when you sell the property, they will gain returns again.

Fifth Circle of Influence
The fifth circle of influence is accessible as you join clubs. The local real estate investment clubs, meetup groups, Toastmaster International groups and the Chamber of Commerce are all groups in which you can potentially network with people from your community. You also have a local Better Business Bureau, perhaps, and you want to talk to them in your continued effort to broaden your circles. I love Toastmasters International because they can teach you to present yourself and your ideas, - skills like how to talk with your body language, your eyes, your mouth, and your enthusiasm.

A bonus is that, as you learn from them, you will also make friends with other members, and the members are mostly investors, entrepreneurs, business owners! They have breakfast group meetings, as well as lunch and dinner meetings, so you could participate in any one of them. Please look for all the local groups where wealthy people meet and talk about investing. Philanthropy organizations are also a very good place to join, contribute and build relationships.

The Elevator Pitch

Having your own short, well thought out introduction will do two things:

1. Make it easier for others to know what you do

2. Make others more interested in you

As you identify your circles of influence and as those circles continue to grow, you absolutely must have the *all-important* **elevator pitch.** Maybe you already know what I'm talking about, but I will explain. When you get on an elevator - in a hotel, an office building, a hotel, anywhere - and there are others on it with you, you have a captive audience for the time it takes to go to either your floor or theirs. There is nowhere anyone can go to escape. Think about your sales pitch as something you could communicate in that limited amount of time.

Obviously, you are not going to be actively recruiting investors in an elevator- (although, it is possible), but fine-tune your sales pitch for your syndicate so that you can deliver it so succinctly that you could present it between floors while riding with someone on an elevator. Regardless from which *circle of influence* your opportunity comes, be

PLATE #2 – BUILDING LISTS AND RELATIONSHIPS · 69

ready on the fly to pitch your deal. Maybe it is with a relative over Sunday lunch or with a local investor you run into in the lobby at the bank. No matter, a quick pitch is sometimes all it takes to open a door to a future deal.

My Elevator Pitch

"Hi, I'm Vinney, and I'm always looking for equity partners to invest in commercial real estate with my company. We look for the assets that have a value play and a momentum play, which means immediate cash-flow right now from the rents, as well as profits, which we share with investors, like you, when we sell the asset. If you are interested in learning more, let's set up a time that we can meet and talk in more detail and see if this is something for you. Even if it turns out not to be right for you at this time, it never hurts to explore the possibilities."

Moving Beyond Resistance and Rejection

As we have already established, investors are skeptical by nature. And why wouldn't they be? It is, after all, their hard-earned money that they are investing with you in the syndication deal, and it could likely be tied up from three to seven years. That's a lot of time to tie up someone else's money. They need assurance that their 50, 100, 200, or 300 thousand dollars they are going to sink into your idea is going to give them the kind of returns they desire and that you are assuring they will see.

To help your potential investors fairly assess the risk to reward in your deal, you will need to answer all of their concerns and thoroughly explain the numbers and benefits to them. Among the data that will be most important to them are the facts about why the emerging market you chose is the right place and why this is a smart deal in which they should invest. You must keep lots of ammunition of backup data and statistics ready to use in defense of their concerns and possible objections. That's when you will then begin to move beyond the rejection of your deal to a position of openness to learn more about it.

How to Handle Investor Resistance and Rejection

Identify the reasons for rejection
If there is a recurring pattern of rejection, the problem may be in your presentation.

Keep in mind that one rejection is not a setback. You move on to other potential partners, and you thank the uninterested party for his or her time. However, if rejection becomes a pattern, then you need to reevaluate some things about your deal. It could mean that you have not adequately covered those things in your presentation that are most important and reassuring to investors. You may be well-versed in your knowledge of the deal, but perhaps you are not showing them everything you know, or maybe they have simply misunderstood despite your best efforts.

Never argue with your potential investors
Conflict with an investor will seldom result in closing the deal.

Never place your investors on the defensive side of the deal. You will never convince them to join you in the syndicate by arguing. It is highly possible that you may not be getting good, reliable feedback from a potential investor. Technically, investors have no legal obligation to tell you the truth. They may offer this reason or that, but, for your own future reference, you do want to try to ascertain the real reason why they are not able or willing to invest with you in your deal. Are they not sold on your team? Do they question your qualifications? Is your tone as good as you say it is? Do they see your vision for the deal clearly?

Seek to understand the investor's confidence level in your team
Investors will pay attention to your team's ability to perform and deliver results. Prove you are as good as you say you are!

Do they see your presence if they Google you? What impression will they have from that search? Do you have a website? And don't forget about your social media presence. Does it help convince them that you,

PLATE #2 – BUILDING LISTS AND RELATIONSHIPS · 71

personally, are not a risky investment? Remember, they are actually giving their hard-earned money, from the nest egg they have put away for retirement, and you must make sure that you are able to show them that you are worth trusting in this business venture. They might be approached with bigger opportunities for investment. You are not the only deal in town, but you want to show them why you are the one to choose to invest in. So, you must work to overcome any rejection with a clear and visible demonstration of why your deal is different and better than others.

As you strive to preparedly handle investor rejection, consider the following:

1. Prepare a STRONG educational brochure for your investors.

2. Include all the exhibits, documentation, Private Placement Memorandum (PPM), Operating Agreement, Subscription Agreement, etc., that will sell them on this deal.

3. Present your deal (maybe through a webinar) to your preexisting relationship potential investors, answering all of their concerns and presenting the benefits of your deal.

4. Market your deal to potential investors. You can only do this in Regulation D exemption, 506 (C).

When it just speaks, sparkles, and shines, you can feel confident about it, and they can tell other people about it. With my people, it has been amazing. I raised $1.9 million in ten days many years back when I was starting out. The way I did that was to put the packet together without any flaws, without any problems. Everything an investor would want to know was carefully laid out in proper fashion with all the exhibits, documents, the PPM, the name and brief resume of our syndication attorney. I actually sent this out to our existing pre-relationship investors, and they were able to see the difference clearly. I conducted two webinars that were very self-explanatory, and I sent out emails. In my emails, I always provide snippets and pictures of the investment right up front and give investors the story behind each. Fortunately, now after many years of experience and with a built-up track record, I can raise $6 to $10 million in a week's time frame. It's sweet.

There are techniques to marketing yourself, so you can put together the right deal. We have been challenged on our assumptions many times, by the way. Are they believable? We could pitch the deal with lots of very lucrative-sounding assumptions - about the increase of rents and revenues and reduction of expenses and all those things, but the investors are savvy. They want to really look through it and say, "Is this guy just blowing smoke, or is it really as good as it seems?" Some may not believe the projections of the huge growth rate and the returns that you are promoting in the investment packet. And that is fine. You never want to guarantee anything. Always remember, and make sure your investors do, too, that these are all projections with the market timing and everything in your experience that you are showing in the PPM package and product. Barring any unforeseeable market shifts, your projections should come to fruition.

Investors sometimes think you are receiving excessive fees in the deal
You have the right, as the syndicator, to take an Acquisition Fee. You should share in the cash flow and equity of the deal.

Are you taking too much of a fee or an unfair share of other expenses? I always hear that. Some investors, not that many--but some, do ask why you are charging 5% of the deal. I just closed with a 5% acquisition fee, and that would be pretty nifty money - almost $300,000. That's not a bad payday, but your investors need to see that, even after taking that acquisition fee, their own returns in the deal are also spectacular. In this deal, I am taking 40% as manager of the cash flow equity and giving 60%. **However, the investors are still going to come out soaring with about 22% to 24% return per year, after taking care of closing**

PLATE #2 – BUILDING LISTS AND RELATIONSHIPS · 73

costs, additional expenses, and escrows. I definitely want to mention here as the market has gotten hotter, the sales prices have soared as I am finishing this book in the first quarter of 2019, the splits have to be reconsidered for syndication purposes. Many times now you have to do an 80/20 or 70/30 split to really get the right yearly preferred rate for the investors and one may have to take only 3% acquisition fee instead of 4 or 5%. Then the syndicator/ managing group will add value-adds to increase rents and decrease expenses to increase the NOI (Net Operating Income).

Investors are information-savvy
They will ask you many questions; listen carefully to all they say and provide answers.

See, the investor community is quite inquisitive and savvy, and we must give them the respect due, as well as the opportunity to ask questions. When they do, listen to them! Be quiet and listen. Learn to read between the lines and assume questions they are not even asking. I always tell my teams, "Slow down to speed up!" You must! If you, instead, are really running and gunning and speeding and talking fast, and investors are not understanding you, guess what? They will have lots of unanswered questions at the end.

So, don't hurry. Don't push them toward an acquisition about which they are confused, because confused investors never invest! Write it down. It is always difficult to try to clear up their confusion once they have become confused the first time. So, work to avoid confusion in the pitch from the very beginning.

Don't Be Desperate
Desperation is easy to sense, it makes investors uneasy, and it causes investors to shy away from you and your deals.

If investors feel you are too desperate, they will wonder what it is about the deal that makes you so anxious and why you are trying to push them so hard to invest money in it. We tell all of our people to show the investors the entire syndication package: the PPM, the operation agreement, the subscription booklet, the property investment brochure, all financial data, occupancy, and much more. We go a step further, and we show all of this, also, to their attorneys and CPAs, and we do it with great confidence so that they can be totally given to investing in the deal. We want all of the counsel they will seek to wholeheartedly agree, "Yes! This is a good deal!" We, especially, focus on providing all of this to the managers of the self-directed IRAs. You have to do this in an effort to provide them all that they need to look at it and see that you are the real deal. They need to be 100% sold on this investment, and if they are, then they won't reject you or your deal. If it is a foolproof deal, they won't reject it!

Pay Attention to the Feedback
If you are receiving the same negative feedback from multiple investors, rethink your strategy and approach.

If a lot of feedback is given from your investors regarding the same issues, there must be an area to which you should give further attention. They can't all be wrong, can they? Maybe it is just an area you have not thoroughly explained, or maybe you need to rethink that one issue and get answers to solve those concerns.

Challenge yourself! Maybe what you have put together so far is not such a great investment package. Improve upon it, and present it again with new information, new evidence to back up your data, new studies to assure your growth, and new numbers demonstrating the value being added to the investment and the reduction in expenses. All of these items, when put together, make an airtight syndication package. Quantify and qualify all of the materials, present them slowly and thoroughly, and you will win them over.

PLATE #2 – BUILDING LISTS AND RELATIONSHIPS · 75

How to Use Other People's Money (OPM)

I would like to talk now about money, specifically how to get OPM (other people's money - isn't that a great acronym?). This is a subject we must discuss in our efforts to be prepared and to overcome that fear of asking the investors to share their money with you!

Money is a sensitive subject. It really is. People do not want to part ways with the money they worked hard to earn and save. Borrowing from that last tenet in *dealing with rejection*, I cannot stress enough that we, the syndicators, truly must put ourselves in the investors' shoes.

Put Yourself into Your Investors' Shoes
Scrutinize your own deal as though you were one of the investors (after all, you are!).

Try to understand what is left unclear that might lead to rejection.

- Why would I invest my money in the deal?
- What are the returns and the risks?
- Is this syndicator (or team) as good as they say? I have to check that!
- What is my risk tolerance?

This is the question: *Why would I invest my hard-earned money, my retirement money, with me?* That's a valid question. Why would I? That is, after all, what your investors are asking. The answers you provide to this question will really be the key to overcoming objections and fear among your potential investors and getting them happily involved in your syndication plans.

- What are the returns?
- What are the risks involved?
- Would I lose my money?

Investors are probably thinking about these questions and more. They will research you! They will double check on your integrity, your track record, as well as the record of your team. They will want to talk to previous investors and contacts. I know all of this from personal experience; this is what really has happened with me and my company and my investors. Investors are very much skeptical. What's my risk tolerance?

At this point, it helps to focus on accredited investors. They are mature and have invested money in real estate deals before. They know quite a bit about the types of investments from their experience investing in the stock market and their entrepreneurial endeavors. They have a good net worth, and they understand the risks.

The Securities and Exchange Commission (SEC) laws are very strict, and it is our fiduciary responsibility to partner with people who know the real risks that are involved in syndication. You want some of your investors to be knowledgeable, people who read the *Wall Street Journal,* and other publications like that.

At this point in the deal, you may find it advantageous to be choosey, selecting carefully those you allow to enter into your syndications. Remember, this is a three-to-seven-year relationship with them and with their money with your LLC/LP or entity. Can you hold them? Can you work with them? Would they be a pain, or would they be pleasant to work with? Would they be flooding you with tons of questions every day, week, and month?

Personally, I have been blessed by the people with whom we have partnered. I do send lots of different articles, and I work hard to keep them abreast with our company's Profit and Loss (P&L) statements, the Rent Rolls (RR), the occupancy units, the Capital Improvement reports and schedules, the Monday Morning Reports (MMRs), delinquencies, marketing plans, and whatever else they may want. We give them access to the ledgers; we can send bank statements to our investors. Transparency

PLATE #2 – BUILDING LISTS AND RELATIONSHIPS · 77

is the right thing to do, and, by sharing that with the prospective investors, they will feel good about doing business with us. Being forthright about all the things happening in your syndication process is a must. Investors like the idea that they will not be ripped off or kept in the dark. They will enjoy and appreciate being close to the heart of the business.

Go for the right deal

- Choose the right emerging market
- Underwrite the deal
- Pre-qualify for the loan, get a loan sponsor to increase net worth requirement
- Properly inspect the property
- Prepare the right syndication package

So, the panacea, the real solution, is for the whole investment to be in the right emerging market, to be well underwritten, to be well-inspected, to be properly put together and packaged. Syndications can be much easier that way, and you will be able to really enjoy the whole process of it. A significant personal investment (many times called "skin in the game") into an attractive, successful proposal is really a compelling way to convince investors to buy in.

You will find it advantageous to do this a little at first. Ultimately, we figured out a way syndicating in which we only have to invest little money, and most of the money is raised out of the investment - the down payment, the closing cost, the escrows, the due diligence, the acquisition fee, EVERYTHING is raised into the equity. We were told by our syndication attorneys when we were starting out; that as long as the deal numbers made sense about monthly or quarterly cash flows and equity gains for Investors, we only needed to buy our interest by putting very little down. My partner and I decided to put only $1,000 and a lot of sweat equity and taking a lot of risks by signing on the loans plus taking the full responsibility of managing the assets all throughout the possession of it till disposition. Now, of course, we do see lenders requiring for the sponsors to put more into the deals, more skin in the game. So, make sure that you have a good track record behind you, at least your own seed money into it if possible. Prepare for questions, provide references, and know all of your numbers and significance of assumptions, as well as why you took them.

Property package presentation

- Be organized
- Answer all the questions
- Know the material really well
- Prove your statement

If this is going to be your first syndication deal, then you have no references from past deals to provide. Instead, provide your investors with recommendations from professional colleagues that you have worked with in the past. Their good word on your behalf can really be a worthwhile inclusion to provide a feeling of confidence and trust from your investors as you endeavor to obtain OPM from them.

Don't be desperate for money!

- Investors must feel comfortable giving you their money
- Do not pressure anyone in investing in any deal

In addition, you can't need the money too much. Let me really stress that. Your potential investors must feel comfortable. They must feel certain that this is the right thing for them to do. So, they need to really look at the deal from every single angle and then feel at peace with the investment. You really cannot push or appear desperate. It is possible to need the money too much, and, when that is the case, investors can smell desperation. If they do, they are going to be running away rather than giving you their money and investing with you in your deal.

Dedicate time and commitment

- Spend time networking

PLATE #2 – BUILDING LISTS AND RELATIONSHIPS · 79

- Take potential investors to lunch/dinner
- Put constant effort to build a stable pool of investors

You must be willing to make a commitment to this venture. Part of the role of syndicator is negotiation, and that often takes place repeatedly over lunches and dinners. This will mean time away from family as you get to know these investors. On the upside, though, you will find that they, too, sort of become an extended family - definitely friends as you are able to gain their confidence and make sure that they are satisfied at each step in the process.

Your goal really is to gain both their trust and their money, and you have the fiduciary responsibility to look out for their investments with your company. Always be selling the deals you are working on. You want to keep your investors apprised of new things that are happening in the marketplace. People like to do business with successful people. The thing that I have done, and what I try to focus on, is always put my investors first. You have to put them first. In order to be successful, you have to find the win for that investor, and you have to look at how you are going to make that profit for them after you have made that win.

Deliver Results

- If you deliver the results you projected, investors will love you for it and continue to invest in the future
- Delivering result will bring you more investors

The more the results of the deals line up with the projections that touted to your investors, the more confidence they will gain in you, and they will definitely tell other people about you. From there, things will really begin to spiral upward. So, remember, it's not just what you project; it's how you deliver, how you manage those assets and provide them the returns they hoped for. From that, you will gain that track record that you can send out to future investors so that they can really feel good about doing business with you.

The Presentation

Let's talk now about public speaking and its challenges as you ready yourself to present your whole packet of syndication to the qualified investors. Some might say that I am not an eloquent speaker. As a matter of fact, I am quite shy, and if you were to ask a lot of people in this world what their biggest fear is, they would say public speaking. They just dread getting in front of people. Most everyone is apprehensive about this until they are able to rehearse and rehearse. I even recommend reciting in front of the mirror so that you are able to see for yourself how to control your body language, balance the inflection in your, and communicate to your audience with your eyes, your face, and your hands.

No matter how uncomfortable public speaking is for you now, you can become a great speaker. What really helps is to thoroughly know your material, including the benefits of your syndication deal, the returns to the investors (the numbers and ratios), and the answers to their questions even before they ask them. Full preparation like that will help it all come together.

So how do you actually deliver winning sales presentations? You have the syndication proposal for the investors, and you know that it exceeds their wildest dreams, and you are so excited about the fact that it will result in great payoff for everyone involved...if only you are able to present it to the investors in a clear, professional, and convincing way! Your deepest desire is that they will be begging you to accept their offers to invest. Wouldn't that be great?

There is, however, a little more work to do to make the sale. You also need to establish the value of the whole package that you have put together by presenting the benefits. I keep saying *benefits,* but the truth of the matter is that the investors do want to see why they should invest with you *or* how and why it is beneficial for them to do so.

PLATE #2 – BUILDING LISTS AND RELATIONSHIPS · 81

How you are going to make the convincing pitch? The ironclad argument? You must show them all of the good returns with the least amount of risk. The secondary goal of this whole step is to create a desire among them to invest with you now. That's the thing! Investors will say things like, "I will catch the next deal." That's not what you want; you want them to invest right now because this is the deal for which you have less than 45 days to raise all the money. You need to act fast and have a good list of a lot of investors with whom you have already have a good relationship. Otherwise, the closing of the deal will be somewhat difficult when the time comes.

People retain

- 20% of what they hear
- 50% of what they see
- Up to 90% of what they touch or feel

People retain only 20% of what they hear...just 20%. However, they retain 50% of what they see and up to 90% of what they touch or feel. The tangible...that's what they remember, what they keep! This means that you have to craft your verbal presentation to specifically match their needs and desires so that within that 20% they do remember will be the information needed to make an investment decision in the right way. So, your presentation really must be good!

Seeing really is believing, so colorful pictures of the investment real estate, collages of images and statistics, PowerPoint or other multimedia presentations all go a long way in providing visualization of the reality of the deal. Emotion is often a key factor in the decision-making process, but you must go beyond just emotion with this savvy group of investors.

What is this deal going to accomplish for each of them in three years, five years, particularly in comparison with the stock market, other real estate deals, or in CDs in or money market accounts? Go beyond just the emotional sales pitch, because logic exists to justify emotional decisions. Make it appealing both emotionally and logically.

How to Deliver a Winning Sales Presentation

1. The presentation
   - Your investment proposal must exceed the investor's expectations
   - Establish the package value by presenting the benefits

2. Create Urgency
   - You want to have investors invest with you NOW
   - Look for the Emotional Benefits of the investment you are presenting

The emotional appeal must be there. If an investor does not feel the connection, you have lost the opportunity to get them happily involved in your investment. No amount of logical, rational debate will counter the effect of not feeling your passion for the deal. Try to connect beyond the individual investor. Get his or her spouse, family involved. Make sure that they are really right there with you to ask you anything and everything about the syndication deal.

Pay Attention To...

1. Your Voice
   - How you say anything is as important as what you say
   - The tone of the voice communicates how you feel

2. Body Language
   - The way your body moves is a statement of your emotions
   - Move around and interact with the audience

3. Appearance
   - Dress Appropriately

How you say it is as important as *what* you say. The content is important, but your delivery is, in some ways, even more important. Your

PLATE #2 – BUILDING LISTS AND RELATIONSHIPS · 83

tone and the volume of your voice can communicate your own belief in and passion for the deal, and they can drive the point across to your audience. Look into their faces; make eye contact, give levels to your volume, and call some of your clients directly by name as you present to them. With permission, share the names of some of your other happy clients. Don't plant yourself in one place for too long but move around to interact with the audience throughout the presentation.

Be prepared. Rehearse the presentation in front of the mirror. Make sure you have dressed appropriately for the audience to whom you are going to speak. If most people are going to be wearing jeans, then dress casually, but do not wear jeans. I suggest a nice shirt, a fresh pair of cotton slacks - just a notch above the dress of the crowd.

Though public speaking is not the focus of this book, it is, as you can see, a critical key to getting the investors to sign on to the deal. While we will move on from this now, keep practicing toward perfection in your presentations. You might even look into a public speaking course at a local college. Trust me, it will be worth the time and money you spend there. After all, if you cannot deliver your message, your dream will remain only a dream.

Be Prepared!

1. Rehearse your 'elevator pitch'
    *   Try rehearsing in front of the mirror!

2. Dress appropriately
    *   Wear casual business attire (no jeans)
    *   You want to be dressed slightly better than the crowd

3. Talk slowly
    *   People want to understand what you are saying so talk slowly
    *   Be calm and talk with conviction

How Many Investors Do I Need?

1. Make it a habit to continuously talk to investors!
2. Investors must fill out all the paperwork before transferring any money.

It is very important to have more investors interested in working with you than you will actually need. On some deals, you will need double the number you assumed you needed to actually close a transaction. It happens for our company; it will happen to yours. On one deal, we had a least fourteen investors who had expressed interest in the next commercial real estate property we would bring in. In the end, though, for multiple reasons, only seven investors showed up with the money. Fortunately, more investors had filled out all the paperwork. Had it not been for them, we would have had to get a "tough money" loan to close the deal. It is so important that you keep many people interested in your investment in the emerging market by building those relationships with the investors even before you have something really good to offer them.

Types of Investors

There are three types of investors for the deals we put together. They are Accredited Investors, Sophisticated Investors, and Suitable Investors.[1]

Accredited Investors

Under the Securities ACT of 1933:

Company that offers or sells its securities, must register the securities with the SEC or find an exemption from the registration requirements. The ACT provides companies with a number of exemptions, for some of the

---

[1] DISCLAIMER: In this segment only part of the SEC regulations and requirements will be covered. Please make sure to check all the details with your security specialist (syndication attorney)!

PLATE #2 – BUILDING LISTS AND RELATIONSHIPS · 85

exemptions such as the rules 505 and 506 of Regulation D, a company may sell its securities to what are known as accredited investors.

Accredited investors as per Rule No. 501, Regulation D of the SEC Regulations

- Bank
- Insurance company
- Registered investment company
- Business development company
- Small Business investment company
- Charitable organization
- Director or executive partner in a company
- Business where all owners are accredited investors
- Actual person

The federal securities laws define the term "accredited investors" in rule No.506 of regulation D of the SEC as a bank, insurance company, registered investment company, business development company or small investment company. Employee benefit plan. These are the stipulations for accredited investors. Charitable organization, cooperation partnerships with assets exceeding $5,000,000. They can also participate as accredited investors. The director or executive partner of the company. Business where all the owners are accredited investors can come into an investors review. An actual person.

Since actual persons are the ones to whom we are pitching our deal, the definition is of particular interest. An actual person, who would be considered an Accredited Investor, is one who has an individual net worth, with his or her spouse, that exceeds $1,000,000 at the time of the purchase of the security. They cannot include their primary residence acuity into their net worth of $1,000,000. That first option could exclude a lot of would-be investors for our deals. But, the second option broadens our investor pool. An actual person, who would be considered an Accredited Investor, is someone with an annual income (for the last

2-3 years) exceeding $200,000, or with a joint income with their spouse exceeding $300,000.

Sophisticated Investors

Type of investor who is deemed to have sufficient investing experience.

They need to demonstrate that they have investing knowledge:

- Have received investing education in the past
- Have invested in real estate before
- They know the risks involved with investing in multi-family

The sophisticated investors are those who are deemed to have sufficient investing experience. They must weigh the risk and the merits of an investment opportunity. They must be able to prove to you that they are knowledgeable, that they have been investing in real estate, and that they know the risks involved (they have been to seminars, courses or boot camps). These factors will determine if they are sophisticated investors.

For certain purposes, the net worth and the income restrictions must be met before the person can be classified as a sophisticated investor. You need to find out if the distinction makes an investor eligible to buy into certain investment opportunities, such as IPO securities that are considered as non-disclosure or non-prospective issues. In most cases, our syndication attorneys say that the sophisticated investors should be about 35 years old. However, they need to have broad knowledge and experience in real estate and investments and be aware of the risks. It is a good practice to ask for copies of their portfolios detailing their experience prior to your deal.

Suitable Investors

Ways to determine if investors are suitable

1. Is your investment aligned with the investor's goals?
2. Can they afford to lose their money?

PLATE #2 – BUILDING LISTS AND RELATIONSHIPS · 87

Of all of the types, the "suitable investor" is, perhaps, the most important to us. A syndicator must have the ability to determine if investors are suitable for an offering. Specifically, if the investment opportunity being offered matches the investors' investment goals and if they can afford to lose the money, then they are *suitable.* If the answer, however, is NO, the syndicator should not take the investors' money. The PPM speaks specifically about the risks involved in the syndication process, in the investments. How illiquid is the money? The investors, themselves, can help you determine if they are suitable or not. They need to know that their money is put into security for three-to-seven years. Give them access to your attorneys, as well as their own. Let them consult with CPAs, financial advisors, family, and friends

Coming in for the Landing

Remember the *Elevator Pitch?* That is the basic introduction. It involves the simple explanation that you buy commercial real estate in emerging markets, that you produce good cash flow and strong back-ends (back-end is the equity gain when the building is sold), and that you will be willing to give your partners an EQUITY position and not a DEBT position. A debt position would be if you borrowed the money at a simple interest rate and pay back the investors. That is not what we are doing. We are giving them an equity position, sharing the cash flows with them, as well as a portion of the equity gains when we sell the property. After this short introduction, some people will be interested in knowing more.

Here are some key phrases to throw into your conversation. They might be different for you, but the results should be the same because you are peaking their interests. The key phrases you want to use are:

"We take a conservative approach." People like to hear that you are proceeding with caution and to be given a very detailed plan, in writing, about the project you undertake.

"If you are interested, I give my investors the majority of the cash flow and the majority of the equity. I want you to have a lot of incentive to participate in my deals." You have placed the focus on what the investor will gain by participating. This puts the focus on them and their interests, rather than on you.

"We only buy in areas where there is a predictable path of progress, where jobs are coming, and where the new businesses are moving. We do a lot of research with the local Chamber of Commerce, economic development groups, and the U.S. Census Bureau. They provide us lots of extensive information that we have used to identify where we are going to acquire our investments." This demonstrates that you have done your homework and are prepared. Investors will appreciate the fact that you are not just pitching your "good idea" to them but that you are, in fact, presenting them with a well-prepared plan for a profitable investment.

Key Follow-up Phrases

"We take a conservative approach."

"If you are interested, I give my investors the majority of the cash flow and the majority of the equity. I want you to have a lot of incentive to participate in my deals."

"We only buy in areas where there is a predictable path of progress: the jobs are coming, where the new businesses are moving in...And we do a lot of research with the local Chamber of Commerce, Economic Development Groups, US Census Bureau. They provide us lots of extensive information that we have to use to identify where we are going to acquire our investments."

PLATE #2 – BUILDING LISTS AND RELATIONSHIPS · 89

"We like to buy B & C properties in A & B areas."

"Exit strategies: value Play, momentum play, etc." value play is when you renovate the building in order to increase the value of the property. Momentum play is when the cash is already flowing, and you can start paying cash flows to the investors from day one of operation. This is not a deal in which you are repositioning, and the investors will have to wait six months to a year before they receive some kind of cash flow. This momentum play is already working. We can start paying them the cash flows. And, if the property is 90% or 95% occupied, you have the ability to increase the value of the investment.

"We typically want to be in and out of the market place within three to five years, depending on where we come in the cycle and that is the emerging cycle."

This communicates that you feel a sense of duty and urgency about providing them a full return on their investment. They will likely go for it since this is not an extremely long commitment.

Handling Objections

You have no need to handle any objections until your investors have signed the **Investor Accreditation Form.** Just like a residential real estate agent wants to know if he is dealing with qualified buyers, you want to know if potential investors have the money and other qualifications to actually close the deal with you. Again, as you seek to establish a relationship, this step is worth the effort.

Oh, and they will start to ask questions! How much do I need to participate in your investment? What kind of returns are you paying? How much money can I make? The investors ask these questions.

My response is always the same: *"Since our company is SEC compliant, we follow all the rules and regulations put forth by the SEC. What*

I would like to do is send you the Accredited Investor Form. Once I receive it back, signed and dated, I will call you to set up a meeting, and at that time I can answer all your questions. At that meeting, we will discuss all your concerns, and I will answer every question you have."

This is the close. Make sure you get the investor's contact information so that you can send him the Accreditation Form and follow up. Once you have received the form, you have closed one of the most important parts of the deal.

Keep Track

Finally, keep track of every conversation with every contact. You can start an excel worksheet of each potential investor and the meetings you have had with each. Keep getting these people in your database. Keep them close by sending them articles and newsletters and other informative documents.

I rely on graphics, pictures, and charts to capture the clients' attention and make it easier for them to understand my deal. If the investors understand your deal completely, and everything is clearly specified, you will have a better chance of them investing with you.

You Must be Thinking is It

The first thing, you want to tell them is it is a great apartment, in a great city, in a great state. You can display a beautiful picture that can capture their attention.

PLATE #2 – BUILDING LISTS AND RELATIONSHIPS · 91

If you are sending the presentation electronically, do not send it in a regular PowerPoint format. Instead, convert every document to a PDF. This protects you and your presentation from being altered by anyone else along the way. In the agenda, you will be telling them of the investment overview. To it, you can add photos to share. The deal specifics will also be included here: what the deal is about and the investment strategy.

❖ Newly Renovated Multifamily Asset
❖ Fully Stabilized occupancy at 92%
❖ Increase property value by
   ○ Bringing rents to market value (10% below market!)
   ○ New Regional Management to reduce costs
   ○ Annual 4-5% rent growth in this emerging area
❖ City of XXXX strong job market
   ○ Highest manufacturing jobs per capita in the State
❖ Central commuter location to Major City
❖ Quiet, desirable living location outside of Metro
❖ Near golf club, park, and historic downtown of XYZ
➡ ❖ Favorable FNMA financing

In the investment overview; you must include good, solid points about the investment. In this example, we put a newly-renovated multi-family asset, fully established occupancy, increased property value, adding rents to the market value, and annual growth in this emerging area. You should demonstrate proof that yours is an emerging market. Also, insert the city or 'xxxxx' strong market, central commuter location to the major city. Provide a description (quiet, desirable location outside the city, near a golf club, part of the historic downtown of 'xyz,' and favorable FNMA financing).

You should insert the pictures of the property. How it looks from the front, from the swimming pool, from the barbecue area. Here you see that we inserted the swimming pool, the interior of the office, and a variety of other views your investors might want to see.

PLATE #2 – BUILDING LISTS AND RELATIONSHIPS · 93

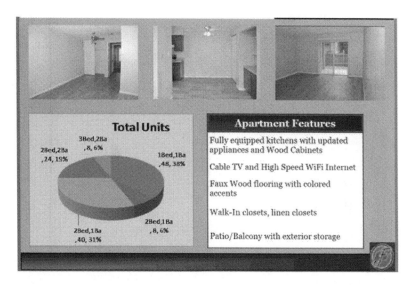

You should also provide photos of the actual units. Investors like to see what they are paying for. Often, they will never be on location to see the actual property. Give them as many images as possible to help them feel connected to their purchase.

Show them the regional map, where it is located and what the freeway is like.

Show them the aerial view of the property.

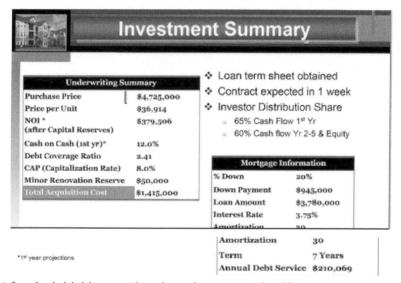

After the initial images that show the property itself, you should go into the investment summary. What is the purchase price? Other values? Take the underwriting details and put them in your presentation to the investors. Show them the CAP rate, minor preservation reserves, and how much you are raising to complete the deal (which is the total acquisition cost). It should show the loan terms sheet, investor-distribution share (that is how much the investors are going to make), the down payment, and other values.

PLATE #2 – BUILDING LISTS AND RELATIONSHIPS · 95

	Year 1	Year 2	Year 3	Year 4	Year 5	
Percent Distributions to Investors	65%	60%	60%	60%	60%	
Managers Cash Flow	$61,722	$84,261	$96,723	$102,434	$106,428	Cash Flow
Investor Cash Flow	$114,628	$126,392	$145,084	$153,651	$159,643	$699,396
Initial Equity Contribution	$1,415,000					
						Total
Investors Cash Flow Return Annualized	8.10%	8.93%	10.25%	10.86%	11.28%	49.43%
Investors Equity Cash Flow at Sale (Yearly prorated)	10.48%	10.48%	10.48%	10.48%	10.48%	52.42%
Investors Total Return On Investment (TROI)	18.59%	19.42%	20.74%	21.34%	21.77%	101.85%
			Cash Flow Returns	Returns at Sale	Total Returns	RETURNS per annum
Investors Return (Cumulative)=			49.43%	52.42%	101.85%	20.37%

Of most importance to the potential investors is the projected cash flow! According to our example included here, in the first year, they are making about 65%, and then the other values for the next five years. We show how much the managers and the investors make, as well as the initial equity contribution. They can see their cash flow return and their equity flow return.

*Note: Depending on the closing, there might be 1-2 months of cash flow returns additional to this. The rates of return displayed on this page are only projections, and are not guarantees of any sort. Actual returns may vary widely, due to many economic and marketplace factors beyond our control.

The disclaimer is very important. We are not guarantors of the rates of return.

		Year 1	Year 2	Year 3	Year 4	Year 5
Revenues						
Gross Scheduled Rents (GSR)		$935,500	$966,959	$1,026,431	$1,062,091	$1,073,135
Vacancy (Avg)	8.0%	$74,840	$78,956	$82,114	$84,967	$85,851
Concessions		$25,656	$24,854	$26,529	$21,042	$21,403
Loss to Lease		9385	$9,269.5	10284.306	10920.9137	10731.3319
Non-Revenue Units		0	0	0	0	0
Rental Income		$823,240	$873,403	$913,528	$956,059	$966,089
Utility Reimbursement		$62,600	$67,108	$71,716	$76,324	$80,902
Other Income		$84,000	$86,520	$89,116	$91,789	$94,543
Total Income		$969,740	$1,027,001	$1,074,955	$1,124,474	$1,139,565
Expenses						
Taxes at Rate of	2.29907%	$86,825	$88,883	$90,437	$92,245	$94,066
Insurance		$18,128	$23,040	$23,040	$23,040	$23,040
Repairs/Maintenance		$44,800	$48,144	$47,535	$48,954	$50,423
General Administration		$16,000	$16,480	$16,974	$17,484	$18,008
Management	4.83%	$38,790	$41,083	$42,974	$44,179	$45,203
Electricity		$183,000	$186,430	$192,023	$197,784	$203,717
Marketing		$8,900	$9,888	$10,185	$10,490	$10,805
Contract Services		$33,690	$24,390	$25,122	$25,876	$26,652

Payroll	$128,080	$131,940	$135,790	$139,908	$144,080
Total Expenses	$344,922	$357,908	$364,878	$396,921	$610,023
Expenses as ratio of Total Income	58%	58%	54%	54%	54%
Net Operating Income (NOI)	$424,818	$459,122	$490,278	$554,554	$814,948
Capital Reserves per door	$303	$38,490	$38,400	$38,400	$38,400	$38,600
Cash Flow After Cap. Reserves		$386,418	$429,722	$451,876	$496,154	$476,380
Debt Service @	3.75%	$210,580	$218,363	$210,689	$210,989	$210,080
Total Cash Flow After Debt Service		$176,348	$210,883	$241,697	$266,664	$256,071

We show the Pro Forma, which is our projection (what we think) of what will happen to the asset over the years. We also show the total cash flow.

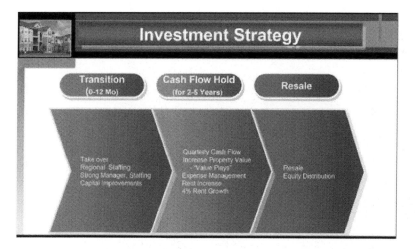

The investment strategy highlights each step in the process in very general terms. It describes the transition period as we are taking over the property and employing managers and regional staffing. This all takes place in the first few months. The Cash Flow Hold is about 2-5 years, during which time investors will see quarterly cash flow, increased property value, expense management, and rent increases by 4%, and so on. Resale is the period of equity distribution. When we sell it, we will be able to give the investors the initial capital, a potential exit strategy, and/or a plan to refinance the property and give the investors their money back.

PLATE #2 – BUILDING LISTS AND RELATIONSHIPS · 97

The Capital Improvements image shows what the seller has already contributed to the property. It shows that $850,000 in renovation was completed- many units were upgraded, the roof was replaced, the pool was renovated, etc. We want to analyze what the seller has done with the money.

NOI at the end of 5th year		$514,540
Exit Price at end of 5th year at CAP	8.1%	$6,391,806
Sales Expense	4%	$255,672
Closing Costs	1%	$63,918
Initial Loan Principal		$3,780,000
Principal Pay down		$359,025
Owner Equity		$2,651,240
Less Initial Investment		$1,415,000
Owner Equity Creation		$1,236,240
Manager's share of equity ->	40%	$494,496
Member Net Equity Share ->	60%	$741,744
Member Net Equity as % of Initial Investment		52.42%
Member Net Equity Growth per Year		10.48%

Then, you want to show them the exit strategy. At the end of the fifth year, what will be the NOI and other values (according to projections)?

Finally, you will display the GOING FORWARD ACTIONS plan. You want to have this slide. It shows the investors the steps that will follow this presentation. This should be presented at the end of the deal. You do not want people to take the deal from under you. You want to sign non-disclosure agreements. You want to propose 75 days to close, 30 days for due diligence to negotiate or repair credit if necessary, and 45 days to loan approval (already in process). If you are new to syndication, you might consider asking one or a few of your investors if they want to become a loan sponsor in the deal.

PLATE #2 – BUILDING LISTS AND RELATIONSHIPS · 99

Being Prepared!

How much money to raise from an investor

Preparing for the syndication process, there are certain details to which we must attend. The first is the question of how much money we must raise from one investor and why that amount?

It is good to put about $100,000 - $200,000 maximum in a single deal where you are raising about $2,000,000. Most people invest about $50,000-$100,000 in a single deal. They are risking that money because of the syndication process as seen in the PPM. There are risks involved in any investment. You can compare syndication to the stock market or putting the money in a savings account or into mutual funds. The returns are much less impressive, but they are less risky.

Your deal, by comparison, offers much higher returns, about 6-10% yearly cash flow and 8-10% back-end yearly equity gains. At the end of the year, the total investor return is about 14-20% yearly, but there are risks. You have to let them know the risks and ask them if it is the right thing for them to do. Go back to the graphics that explain Accredited Investors, Sophisticated Investors, and Suitable Investors.

As a syndicator, you have responsibilities and legal restrictions on who you can involve in your deal. In the PPM, you can set the minimum and maximum amount an investor can put in one deal. Usually, we take $50,000 for smaller deals and $100,000 if we want to raise about $2 million. It usually takes about 20 people investing $100,000 each to raise $2 million.

It is best to have fewer investors in a syndication deal because it is easier to communicate with a smaller number of investors when it comes to keeping track of them during meetings and other aspects.

What expenses do you incur during a syndication?

Another thing is "what expenses do you incur during syndication process?" Because of your responsibility to your investors, you want them to diversify their risks. In other words, they should not put all their eggs in one basket. This works to your benefit, too, as they invest in different properties.

Some typical expenses are:

1. Earnest Money – 1-2% of the purchase price

2. Due Diligence - $30-35/unit

3. Loan Application Fee - $2,500-10,000

4. Survey Reports (Phase 1)- $4000-7500

5. Appraisal $3,500-$7,500

6. Syndication and Other Legal Fees $15,000-$20,000

You also need to qualify as the loan sponsor for the deal. What are some of the expenses you will incur in the syndication process? If you are buying a 120-unit apartment building in an emerging market, and the purchase price is about $5,000,000, the first thing required of you is the earnest money. Earnest money is paid to the title company within three days of the execution of the purchase and sales contract. It is usually 1%-2% of the purchase price.

The less you can put up for the earnest money, the better, because the money that is not tied up is cash that can be spent somewhere else along the way. In this case, the earnest money is $75,000. If you can negotiate $50,000, that would be even better. Sometimes, in the comparative situation, the lender wants to make sure that you will follow through with the deal, so they ask for a higher amount of money.

PLATE #2 – BUILDING LISTS AND RELATIONSHIPS · 101

Your second responsibility is the due diligence money. After the contract, you have between 21 and 45 days to do your due diligence, depending on what you agreed to with the seller. During this process, you will travel to the property, bring the contractor by to evaluate the work needed, and you will inspect each of the units. This will cost money, and that money is referred to as the *due diligence expenses*. Remember, NEVER PERFORM SPOT CHECKING! This is when you only view some of the units, maybe 30 or 60 units out of 120 you are purchasing. You must check every unit. Sometimes the seller's agent/broker or the seller's property manager will show you just the good units. They may not offer to show you the bad units, and then, when you have closed the deal, you find out what you did not know, and nothing can be done. So, during the due diligence process, hire a general contractor to check the property thoroughly...maybe even two! You will receive a detailed report of the property and what needs to be repaired or changed. This report will be part of your syndication package. You need to disclose everything to the investors. The due diligence is usually $30-35/unit.

Your third responsibility or cost is the Loan Application Fee. It is usually about $2,500-$10,000. The lender broker will ask for this fee. The Loan Application fee needs to be available from the very beginning because we like to close in 60 days, and several processes have to start right away. Once the property has been thoroughly checked, you can start the loan process with the lender and pay the money to the syndication attorney.

Once you know you are going to go ahead with the purchase, then you can start giving money out for the third-party inspection reports, survey reports, and appraisals. This can cost about $5,000-$7,500.

All of the syndication fees are paid upfront by you, the syndicator, to get the syndication process started. You can raise this money from your loan sponsor or use your own funds. Syndication and other legal fees can be $15,000-$20,000 (about $15,000 for the syndication fee and a few thousand dollars for entities, LLCs, and lawyer fees). The total amount for syndication expenses is a huge amount. It totals about $115,000 to $120,000. You need this money up front just to get the process started. All these expenses will be reimbursed to you, as specified in the PPM.

The investors must fill out all the paperwork before they wire the money into the company LLC. It is only when the minimum amount has been raised that we can "break that account." When we "break that account," we use that money to reimburse ourselves and other parties for those upfront expenses. Remember, if you are not able to raise all the funds or close on the commercial assets, you are liable to return all money raised to each investor and you lose all the money that you have spent on the previous expenses.

Since syndicators take this risk all the time during the syndication process, you can see just how important these strong lists of investors are and how necessary it becomes to develop relationships with them along the way. No one wants to be in this deal all alone. You need the investors, and they need you!

Good luck!

CHAPTER FIVE

Plate #3 – Underwriting and Analyzing the Deals

As we begin spinning this third plate, I want you to remember something important. In any deal, you must make the decision to marry the NUMBERS only, not the WAY THE PROPERTY LOOKS!

In the analysis portion of any deal, we must remember that it is the local economy that matters, and that applies to pockets of the area rather than the entire metro market. In this chapter, we are going to talk about emerging markets and market cycles as keys to underwriting and analyzing the very best syndication deals.

Emerging Markets

What is an emerging market? A real estate market that has the potential to appreciate very quickly over a three to five-year period is usually considered as an **emerging market**.

In other words, an emerging market is a real estate market where there are jobs coming in, new companies are sprouting up, the population is growing, new construction is affordable, and demand for apartments is higher. One distinctive characteristic of an emerging market is that it has the potential to give a high return on the investment.

Investing in assets in Emerging Markets gives you the opportunity to benefit from high ROI

Emerging markets are characterized by:

 People migrating in, rather than leaving a geographic area

 Jobs being created rather than lost

 Rents and **property values** quickly **rising**

 Strong, local **government leadership** dedicated to attracting jobs

 Markets beginning to **absorb oversupply**

There are, typically, between fifteen and twenty markets in the United States that are emerging at any given time. There are smaller markets within each state or the province that we can research and discover to also experience a big upswing in growth.

PLATE #3 – UNDERWRITING AND ANALYZING THE DEALS · 105

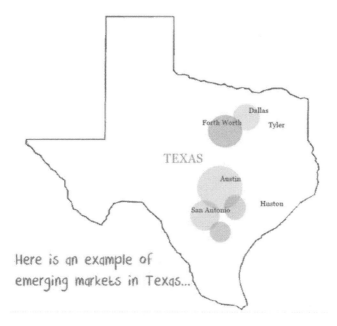

Here is an example of emerging markets in Texas...

Why Emerging Markets?

- Higher than average returns
- Attractive for investors
- Easier to syndicate deals
- Little competition
- NOI increases faster

Why do we concentrate on emerging markets? These are the areas that will bring nice returns for your investors and you. The emerging markets are, therefore, more attractive to the investors creating a more expedient route to financing the deal and a much more appealing route to syndication. The investor money is easier to follow you as you acquire properties in the emerging markets. It is a buzzword when you are raising investor money. It really makes a difference when you are meeting with people and can tell them, "Hey, there is this really nice opportunity in an emerging market."

Always ask your investor about their RISK FACTOR and what locations they prefer to invest in: city, state, etc.

Give consideration to the preferred cities and states in which your investors want to put their money. Fill your "pool" with the investors with whom you want to syndicate. Determine their risk factor! Where would they like to invest money? In what states? What cities? Then look for the emerging markets in those areas. There is very little competition when we are dealing in emerging markets because not too many people know about them. Of course, as the area begins to experience more and more growth, more people will find out about it, but by then you are already syndicated in the area and are, consequently, part of the growth they will discover. You are one step ahead in the race!

In these emerging markets, the NOI (Net Operating Income) grows faster. It is a much quicker way to grow the rates and increase the NOI. For example, in one of the markets in Texas, my company bought an apartment building for $1,950,000, and in just eighteen months, we were able to put it on in the market for $4,200,000. Wow! More than doubling the money was a GREAT return for our investors!

EMERGING MARKET CYCLE

PLATE #3 – UNDERWRITING AND ANALYZING THE DEALS · 107

Take a look at the emerging market cycles (figure above). It is a little like a roller coaster, or even a loop. It starts with Buyer's Market 1, quickly progressing to Buyer's Market 2. Once it moves on from a Buyer's Market 1, we become increasingly interested in that market, thus the next cycle, Buyer's Market 2 is when we want to pick up the property. This approach makes the most sense, as you will see, as we move into the next cycle in the loop, which is the Seller's Market stage? It comes after a buyer's market.

Buyer's Market 1 Overview

- Still oversupply
- Prices and rents are falling
- Time on market increasing
- New construction is stagnant
- Unemployment reaches height
- Foreclosure rises sharply

The Buyer's Market 1 stage is where there is an oversupply; the prices are coming down off of office buildings, apartments, and other commercial properties. Anytime there is an oversupply, prices and rents begin falling. As you know, when prices are falling the NOI falls. When the NOI falls, the prices of the property fall, time on the market increases, new construction is stagnant, and very few people want to build in that market phase. With that oversupply, likewise, unemployment reaches high levels.

When unemployment is high, a great number of people find it difficult to rent out or spend money at the grocery stores. It is just a downward cycle in the market. Foreclosure rises sharply, as we have seen them in the U.S., as well as other parts of the and all over the world. Remember 2007-2009? In times like these, though still a Buyer's Market, you can buy cheaper.

Buyer's Market 2 Overview

- Market absorbs oversupply
- Time on the market decreases
- Job growth increases
- Existing properties are being rehabbed
- Prices and rents begin to slowly increase

In the **Buyer's Market 2 phase,** at the lowest point, the market typically absorbs oversupply. The time on the market decreases, and the job growth is beginning to move back into a mode of increase. Offers are coming into that area. Existing properties are being rehabbed. The prices and the rents begin to increase slowly. That is why we call this stage the *Millionaire Maker.* As the nickname indicates, that is the best time to buy.

Seller's Market 1 Overview

1. Supply dwindles
2. Properties selling fast
3. Time on the market at the lowest point
4. Property price and rent rising
5. Demand at its highest point

What happens next, in the Seller's Market 1, is that the supply dwindles because so many people are buying commercial real estate. The supply goes down while the property is selling faster. As a result, there are fewer properties in the market, whether it is multi-family, industrial companies, offices, hotels, or other commercial properties. Time on the market is at the lowest point, and property and rent rise. Demand is at its highest point. This is the seller's market. Sellers are unable to determine how much they want to sell their properties. There are some bids coming in from a variety of buyers, and that drives the price higher.

Seller's Market 2 Overview

- Time on the market increases

PLATE #3 – UNDERWRITING AND ANALYZING THE DEALS · 109

- Supply increases
- Sellers waiting but still get inflated prices
- Construction is excessive
- Business & job growth are slow

In **Seller's Market 2,** time on the market increases. Supply increases. The seller is waiting but still faces inflated prices. The construction pipeline is excessive. Business in the area and job growth is also slow.

So, you see that the best time to buy actually *is* in the Buyer's Market. You will want to make the purchase, work to increase rents and improve on the property's value for about three to five years. After that, you will be able to sell the property during a Seller's Market 2 phase. I recommend this process so that you can sell it before a downward trend begins, just in case the market is headed over a cliff.

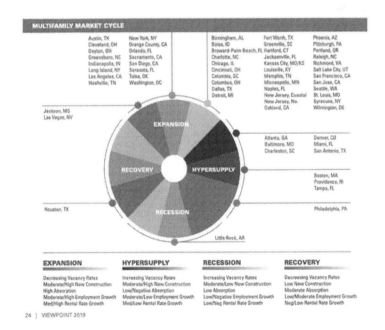

There is a great service provided for properties here in the U.S., called Integra Realty Resources, Inc. (www.irr.com). The above diagram is for 2019 multifamily markets all across the USA in their different phases. This company, according to their own website, provides "comprehensive commercial real estate market research, valuation, and advisory services." Quite a few of their services are available as free resources in the U.S. So much of what we do, as syndicators, relies heavily upon their services because they do considerable work in the fundamental investment-determining phases within these market cycles which includes vacancy rate trends, new product supply delivery, market growth expectations, employment growth statistics, and inventory absorption trends and projections. They design these charts (see figure above), of the market cycles for different states. You can look into the states in which you and your investors have interest to find out where these markets are.

In this particular diagram (Integra Realty Resources, IRR.com 2019), you can view all the phases in any market. Each phase lasts about three to five years, and the span of time between the peaks (top) and troughs (bottom) is about six to eight years. The best time to buy is in the recovery phase. Buyer's market 2 has just happened, and the period is marked by a decrease in the vacancy rate.

Simultaneously, low costs for new construction, moderate absorption, low to moderate employment, and negative or low rental rate growth all contribute to the market's move higher into the expansion stage, in which there is a decrease in the vacancy rate, an increase in rental rates, and a return to moderate-to-high employment rates. There are other agencies that also put out tremendous reports; e.g., for 2019, I have been looking at these: they are Berkadia-2019-National-Apartment-Forecast report, CBRE - Multifamily Resiliency during Recession report, Deloitte US Expectations Market Reality Real Estate 2019, Yardi-Matrix-Monthly-Jan-2019 and other fine economic news publications.

PLATE #3 – UNDERWRITING AND ANALYZING THE DEALS · 111

All my houses went up and down in price in cycles, and so I learned that the key to this business is the market cycles - when to buy and when to sell. In the simplest of terms, you want to buy in the recovery phase and sell in the expansion phase. The tool, also, is to not be greedy by keeping the property for a longer (sometimes too long) time. You have to leave "some meat on the bone" so that other investors who will come along to buy the property can also experience some good appreciation when they are purchasing. You do this so that you do not get stuck with the property far beyond its profitable years.

The worst way to buy properties is in the hyper-supply and the recession phase. Carefully monitor these periods; watch closely. Then, pick up your purchase in the recovery phase right before the Buyer's Market 2. You can still pick it up a little after it, but it is a narrow window of opportunity just before and just after Buyer's Market 2. I will share a little truth with you: you never know where the bottom is until you have gone to the bottom. You look back at it and say, "Oh! That was where the bottom was."

How to Identify Emerging Markets

Do your own market research

1. Job growth reports
2. Population growth reports
3. Path of progress reports
4. Local economy reports and trends
5. Chamber of Commerce reports

Look for the following factors in your market

1. Where are the largest businesses located?
2. How many new jobs are being created?
3. Appealing lifestyle
4. Rental potential
5. State capitals and universities
6. Big box retail and shopping hubs

7. Does your market have an airport?
8. Check out the infrastructure
9. Preferred population of 50-100K

When approaching the emerging markets in the U.S., and all around the world, it is imperative that you conduct the needed market research. You need to look at the job growth reports, the population growth reports, the path of progress reports, local economy reports and trends, and the Chamber of Commerce reports. Try to understand the market in which you are going. We have already discussed Integra (www.irr.com), but several other providers are helpful, too, and you can find much of the information you need within their websites. I like and recommend www.GlobeSt.com and www.cbre.com. There are many reports out there that you will find quite helpful in your process.

Many websites and magazines need to be researched weekly, monthly to find out where the progress is being made in the different parts of the country. Some of them are:

- MULTIFAMILY EXECUTIVE magazine
- Data.gov
- Co-Star.com
- Forbes Magazine
- WallStreet Journal
- Fortune magazine
- U. S. News Top News
- Various podcasts
- Chamber of Commerce of the specific Market
- Commercial brokers of the specific Market
- Property management company of the specific Market

When national attention is focused on a particular market, smart investors are already selling their properties. A common investing mistake is to jump into 'hot' areas as reported on by the press. At any given time – regardless of what the national economy is doing – certain cities are

PLATE #3 – UNDERWRITING AND ANALYZING THE DEALS · 113

in a local expanding cycle, not a 'hot' cycle. Jobs bring markets back to life. For a city to move to the next phase of the market cycle, it must act to grow jobs. When jobs are finally created, people begin to migrate back into a community, population grows, vacant properties start being filled, and rents start to increase. The oversupply stalls markets and triggers the decline of emerging markets.

An investor, like yourself, is wise to look for the emerging markets where the stable, large, and service-oriented industries are coming in. This is a precipitator of new jobs and can jumpstart more appealing lifestyles within the community. There is one segment in San Antonio, which was featured in the *Business Weekly, Fortune Magazine,* and *Forbes.* Because of the lifestyle offered in the area, many young people were moving in that direction. Those are the things that you want to look out for so that you can move into the market quickly and make that purchase. Among other factors to influence your purchase decision are rental potential, proximity to the state capital, and nearby colleges and universities.

You want to look for a market where there are big-box retail stores, shopping malls, and health clubs moving in. These types of businesses, prior to locating in an area, do a lot of extensive market research to see where people will be moving and where the population will be increasing. Then, they choose their market. In addition, these areas are marked by the presence of airports, infrastructures, roads, transportation, and utilities, along with a population no less than 50,000 to 100,000. So, watch the cycles. Stay away from the hyper-supply phases. In the recovery period, when the jobs are coming in, buy these properties.

Net Operating Income (NOI)

Total Income

- Rents
- Coin-operated laundry

- Application fees
- Administrative fees
- Resident reimbursements

Total Income, as the phrase suggests, is the total income that comes from commercial assets. It could be the rent, laundry facilities, Parking fee as well as application and administrative fees for new tenants that are coming in. Likewise, tenant reimbursements for utilities (the extra money that is spent on water or gas) are billed back to the tenant, it's often called RUBS (Ratio Utilities Billing System). Those kinds of revenues will be included in the total income.

One way to increase the NOI is to bill tenants for the water, garbage, and electrical expenses.

Total Income - Operating Costs = NOI

- Real estate taxes
- Insurance
- Maintenance & repair cost
- Management fees
- Payrolls
- Office expenses
- Marketing costs
- Contract services

The NOI is the total income minus the operating expenses. The major operating costs are taxes and insurance. Insurance is a critical part of any income. You should never take less insurance on multi-family housing property, because, when you think you do not need it, you will find that to be the time when you need it most. In addition to the taxes and insurance, you must factor in the maintenance costs (the expense of maintaining the building), including the service manager or, as we call it, the management. Then, add in payroll, office expenses, and marketing costs. All these expenses are taken out, and you are left with the residual of the total income...of the Net Operating Income (NOI).

PLATE #3 – UNDERWRITING AND ANALYZING THE DEALS · 115

Super Investments

Property Information		Date:				1001 SUPER DRIVE
Property Name		THE SUPER INVESTMENT				SUPER CITY, SUPER ZIP CODE
Number of Units	128	Counter Pr:				
Purchase (Strike) Price	$5,125,000	Asking Pr:	$5,300,000		Gross Potential (Market)	$1,107,840
Price Per Unit	$40,039	LOI Price	$4,943,835	93%	Gross Scheduled (Actual)	$1,076,200
Rentable Sq Ft	93,984	Type/ Area:	B/A		Loss to Lease (Upside)	$32,640
Price Per Sq Ft	$64.63	YR Built	1980			

INCOME:		Ours	Per Unit	% of GSR	Sellers	Per Unit	% of GSR	Mortgage Info	
Gross Scheduled Rents(GSR)@100%		$1,275,200	$8,400		$1,002,484	$7,840		Purchase Price	$5,125,000
Physical Vacancy	8.0%	$86,016	$672	8.0%	$60,000	$469	6.0%	% Down	20%
Concessions	1.0%	$12,752	$84	1.0%	$11,198	$87	1.1%	Down Payment	$1,025,000
Loss to Lease	1.5%	$18,128	$126	1.5%	$0	$0	0.0%	Mortgage Amt	$4,100,000
Non-Revenue Units (models, ofc.)		$0	$0	0.0%	$0	$0	0.0%	Interest Rate (AOD 25%)	4.75%
Total Rental Income		$942,304	$2,518	86.9%	$932,381	$7,284	92.9%	AM Term (250yr if int. only)	30
Utility Reimbursement		$15,360	$120	1.4%	$0	$0	0.0%	Annual Debt Service	$256,690
Other Income		$38,000	$297	3.5%	$37,698	$295	3.8%	Interest-Only Debt SVC (YR1)	$194,751
Effective Gross Income		$1,016,664	$7,935	94.5%	$900,989	$7,578	96.7%	Closing/Acquisition Costs	

Expenses:		Ours	Per Unit	% of GSR	Sellers	Per Unit	% of GSR	Closing Costs	1.5%	$61,500
Taxes	2.043141%	$124,269	$811	9.7%	$79,842	$624	8.0%	Loan Points	1.3%	
Insurance		$42,000	$535	3.9%	$65,580	$515	6.6%	Loan Point Cost		$41,000
Repairs and Maintenance		$54,400	$425	5.1%	$58,573	$460	5.9%	Acquisition Fee %		5.0%
General/ Admin		$16,000	$125	1.5%	$22,749	$178	2.3%	Acquisition Fee Amount		$256,250
Management %	4.0%	$40,627	$317	5.8%	$49,102	$384	4.9%	Legal Costs		$16,000
Marketing		$8,600	$75	0.8%	$9,178	$72	0.9%	Total Closing Costs		$374,750
Utility		$75,000	$534	7.0%	$74,345	$586	7.5%	Capital Reserves		$38,400
Contract Services		$35,000	$230	3.3%	$35,203	$275	3.5%	1st Yr Insurance	100%	$42,000
Payroll		$134,400	$1,050	12.5%	$131,340	$1,026	13.1%	Prop Tax Reserve (4 Mo)		$52,334
Total Expenses		$611,298	$3,994	47.6%	$527,912	$4,117	52.5%	Utility Deposit		$15,000
								Repairs/ Maintenance Costs		$102,718

The type of chart above is one that will guide us as we talk about **super investment** in a **super city** on a **super street** in a **super zip code**. This is a multi-family example. It can be applied to storage units and other buildings, too. If it is only one building, the format is a little different. It has many parts to it.

In the example below, we are looking at a 128-unit apartment building, with a strike price of $5,125,000 - this is what we are willing to pay. The asking price is $5,300,000. The LOI price is the price you put down in your Letter of Intent (LOI). We never really pay the full price; we want to negotiate. As I have already said, my philosophy is not to have a buyer's broker. We want to work with the seller's broker and seller directly because there is no vacuum in between. This is the best way to find out what their needs are, and we can make a deal.

Let's use the example above. As we calculate and manipulate the numbers at the bottom of the chart, the strike price changes. We have determined that our strike price is $5,125,000. The price per unit, in this example, is $40,039. The type and Area, in this case, is a B property in an A area. So, it is a good location. Likewise, any time you can get a C property in a B location or a B property in an A location, you've found a good deal. It was built in 1980. The rentable square footage is 93,984. The price per square foot is $54.53.

Property Information		Date:			
Property Name		**THE SUPER INVESTMENT**			
Number of Units	128	Counter Pr:			
Purchase (Strike) Price	$5,125,000	Asking Pr:	$5,300,000		
Price Per Unit	$40,039	LOI Price:	$4,945,625	93%	
Rentable Sq Ft	93,984	Type/ Area:	B/A		
Price Per Sq Ft	$54.53	YR Built:	1980		

Income:		Ours	Per Unit	% of GSR	Sellers	Per Unit	% of GSR
Gross Scheduled Rents(GSR)@100%		$1,075,200	$8,400		$1,003,494	$7,840	
Physical Vacancy	8.0%	$86,016	$672	8.0%	$60,000	$469	6.0%
Concessions	1.0%	$10,752	$84	1.0%	$11,193	$87	1.1%
Loss to Lease	1.5%	$16,128	$126	1.5%	$0	$0	0.0%
Non-Revenue Units (models, offc.)		$0	$0	0.0%	$0	$0	0.0%
Total Rental Income		$962,304	$7,518	89.5%	$932,301	$7,284	92.9%
Utility Reimbursement		$15,360	$120	1.4%	$0	$0	0.0%
Other Income		$38,000	$297	3.5%	$37,698	$295	3.8%
Effective Gross Income		$1,015,664	$7,935	94.5%	$969,999	$7,578	96.7%

Expenses:		Ours	Per Unit	% of GSR	Sellers	Per Unit	% of GSR
Taxes	2.543141%	$104,269	$815	9.7%	$79,842	$624	8.0%

This next part of the worksheet (below) is the seller's actual numbers. You do not want to take the broker's proforma numbers from the Operating Memorandum (OM), as he is apt to dress up the properties and the numbers. The broker has put that together in comparison to other properties in the area. Beware of these BIG proforma numbers, indicating what the property is going to do in five to ten years. What we are looking for are real property numbers - the gross scheduled rents - not their numbers because there is a difference.

PLATE #3 – UNDERWRITING AND ANALYZING THE DEALS · 117

Income:		Ours	Per Unit	% of GSR	Sellers	Per Unit	% of GSR	
Gross Scheduled Rents(GSR)@100%		$1,075,200	$8,400		$1,003,494	$7,840		Purchase Pi
Physical Vacancy	8.0%	$86,016	$672	8.0%	$60,000	$469	6.0%	% Down
Concessions	1.0%	$10,752	$84	1.0%	$11,193	$87	1.1%	Down Paym
Loss to Lease	1.5%	$16,128	$126	1.5%	$0	$0	0.0%	Mortgage A
Non-Revenue Units (models, offs.)		$0	$0	0.0%	$0	$0	0.0%	Interest Rat
Total Rental Income		$962,304	$7,518	89.5%	$932,301	$7,284	92.9%	AM.Term (2
Utility Reimbursement		$15,360	$120	1.4%	$0	$0	0.0%	A
Other Income		$38,000	$297	3.5%	$37,698	$295	3.8%	Interest On
Effective Gross Income		$1,015,664	$7,935	94.5%	$969,999	$7,578	96.7%	
								Closing Cos
Expenses:		Ours	Per Unit	%of GSR	Sellers	Per Unit	% of GSR	Loan Points
Taxes	2.543141%	$104,269	$815	9.7%	$75,842	$624	8.0%	Loan Point (
Insurance		$42,000	$535	3.9%	$65,880	$515	6.6%	Acquisition I
Repairs and Maintenance		$54,400	$425	5.1%	$58,873	$460	5.9%	Acquisition I
General/ Admin		$16,000	$125	1.5%	$22,749	$178	2.3%	Legal Costs
Management %	4.0%	$40,627	$317	3.8%	$49,102	$384	4.9%	
Marketing		$9,600	$75	0.9%	$9,178	$72	0.9%	Capital Res
Utility		$75,000	$586	7.0%	$74,845	$585	7.5%	1st Yr Insur
Contract Services		$35,000	$250	3.3%	$35,203	$275	3.5%	Prop Tax R
Payroll		$134,400	$1,050	12.5%	$131,340	$1,026	13.1%	Utility Depo
Total Expenses		$611,296	$3,994	47.6%	$527,012	$4,117	52.5%	Repair/ Mai
Net Operating Income (NOI)		$504,369			$442,987			Total /
Capital Reserves	$300	$38,400		$300	$38,400	NOTES		

Then, we look at this part, which shows us how many bedrooms and bathrooms we are getting in the units. It also shows us the total number of units and the monthly rent (what they are collecting right now). You can see clearly what the rent is per square foot, as well as what the total rent is, and you can view it either monthly or annually.

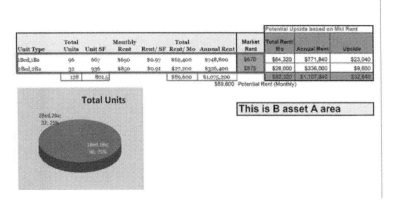

Unit Type	Total Units	Unit SF	Monthly Rent	Rent/ SF	Total Rent/ Mo	Annual Rent	Market Rent	Total Rent No	Annual Rent	Upside
1Bed,1Ba	96	667	$650	$0.97	$62,400	$748,800	$670	$64,320	$771,840	$23,040
2Bed,2Ba	32	936	$850	$0.91	$27,200	$326,400	$875	$28,000	$336,000	$9,600
	128	801.5			$89,600	$1,075,200		$92,320	$1,107,840	$32,640

$89,600 Potential Rent (Monthly)

Potential Upside based on Mkt Rent

Total Units

This is B asset A area

Going back to the previous chart. We list the seller's numbers with the gross scheduled rents, physical vacancy, concessions and others. These combined are our REAL numbers.

Income:		Ours	Per Unit	% of GSR		Sellers	Per Unit	% of GSR	
Gross Scheduled Rents(GSR)@100%		$1,075,200	$8,400			$1,003,494	$7,840		Purchase Pr
Physical Vacancy	8.0%	$86,016	$672	8.0%		$60,000	$469	6.0%	% Down
Concessions	1.0%	$10,752	$84	1.0%		$11,193	$87	1.1%	Down Paym
Loss to Lease	1.5%	$16,128	$126	1.5%		$0	$0	0.0%	Mortgage Ar
Non-Revenue Units (models, offs.)		$0	$0	0.0%		$0	$0	0.0%	Interest Rate
Total Rental Income		$962,304	$7,518	89.5%		$832,301	$7,284	92.9%	AM Term (2!
Utility Reimbursement		$15,360	$120	1.4%		$0	$0	0.0%	A
Other Income		$38,000	$297	3.5%		$37,698	$295	3.8%	Interest On
Effective Gross Income		$1,015,664	$7,935	94.5%		$869,999	$7,578	96.7%	C
									Closing Cost
Expenses:		Ours	Per Unit	%of GSR		Sellers	Per Unit	% of GSR	Loan Points
Taxes	2.543141%	$104,269	$815	9.7%		$79,842	$624	8.0%	Loan Point C
Insurance		$42,900	$535	3.9%		$65,880	$515	6.6%	Acquisition F
Repairs and Maintenance		$54,400	$425	5.1%		$58,873	$460	5.9%	Acquisition F
General/ Admin		$16,000	$125	1.5%		$22,749	$178	2.3%	Legal Costs
Management %	4.0%	$40,627	$317	3.8%		$49,102	$384	4.9%	1
Marketing		$9,600	$75	0.9%		$9,178	$72	0.9%	Capital Rese
Utility		$75,000	$586	7.0%		$74,845	$585	7.5%	1st Yr Insura
Contract Services		$35,000	$250	3.3%		$35,203	$275	3.5%	Prop Tax Re
Payroll		$134,400	$1,050	12.5%		$131,340	$1,026	13.1%	Utility Depos
Total Expenses		$511,295	$3,994	47.6%		$527,012	$4,117	52.5%	Repair/ Main
Net Operating Income (NOI)		$504,369				$442,987			Total A
Capital Reserves	$300	$38,400			$300	$38,400	NOTES		

On our side of the chart, we put down potential prices at $100%, and we see that we are going to get $1,075,200, that is $8,400 per unit, at 8% physical vacancy. Even though this apartment is really in line for underwriting (the lenders will accept it), we want to include that 8% or 10% physical vacancy number to underwrite this property securely. The concessions are about the same on both our side and the seller's side. The loss to lease is $16,128 because not all the units are producing their potential rent. The total rental income is supplemented by the utility reimbursement. This is the amount we bill back to the tenant to recover portions of the utilities. To clarify, we pay the bills to the city utility departments, however, the tenants are billed for some portion of it to reimburse us. In Texas, it is about 90-95%. Other income like vending machines, coin-operated laundry, and other miscellaneous expenses all go into the effective gross income for us, which, in this example is $1,015,664. That's INCOME!

PLATE #3 – UNDERWRITING AND ANALYZING THE DEALS · 119

Expenses:		Ours	Per Unit	%of GSR	Sellers	Per Unit	% of GSR	Loan Points
Taxes	2.543141%	$104,269	$815	0.7%	$79,842	$624	8.0%	Loan Point C
Insurance		$42,000	$535	3.9%	$65,890	$515	6.6%	Acquisition F
Repairs and Maintenance		$54,400	$425	5.1%	$58,873	$460	5.9%	Acquisition F
General/ Admin		$16,000	$125	1.5%	$22,749	$178	2.3%	Legal Costs
Management %	4.0%	$40,827	$317	3.8%	$49,102	$384	4.9%	
Marketing		$9,600	$75	0.9%	$9,178	$72	0.9%	Capital Rese
Utility		$75,000	$586	7.0%	$74,845	$585	7.5%	1st Yr Insura
Contract Services		$35,000	$250	3.3%	$35,203	$275	3.5%	Prop Tax Re
Payroll		$134,400	$1,050	12.5%	$131,340	$1,026	13.1%	Utility Depos
Total Expenses		$511,295	$3,994	47.6%	$527,012	$4,117	52.5%	Repair/ Main
Net Operating Income (NOI)		$504,369			$442,987			Total A
Capital Reserves	$300	$38,400		$300	$38,400	NOTES		
NOI - After Capital Exp		$465,969			$404,587			
Primary Debt Service		$256,650			$219,012	Indiv Elec & HVAC; Water master mete		
Secondary Debt Service		$0			$0			
Cash Flow Before Taxes		$209,318			$185,575			
Cash on Cash Return		12.7%	>12.4%		11.2%	Comments		
Debt Coverage Ratio		1.82	x1.6		1.85			
Cap Rate (Including Capital Exp)			>7.75		8.4%			
Managers Cash Flow		$83,727	40%		$74,230			
Equity Partners Cash Flow		$125,591	60%		$111,345			
COC Return Equity Partners		8.36%			6.75%			
Debt Value (NOI/Debt)		12.3%	>10%					

In the expense column, we put down all the seller's expenses and our numbers. We can see a big change in taxes between them. They must have bought the property a few years ago, which explains the seller's lower taxes of $79,842, as compared to our taxes, which are $104,269. Conversely, their insurance is higher than ours. You can tell how important it is to get different quotes from a few local insurance companies. The policy is always negotiable. Repairs and maintenance are included in the expenses.

Additionally, the general administration fee is lower than that of the seller. The management fee is less than 4%, which is lower than that of the sellers. Marketing and utility fees are included. These are all real numbers that we took from the history of the complex. Contract services like lawn care, swimming pool upkeep, termite prevention, and pest control, etc... The payroll is also added. Altogether, the expenses total for us is $511,295; the seller's total expenses are $527,012. Ours is a little lower, which is good. This is where the NOI comes in. Before the mortgage is taken out, we take the total effective gross income, which in this case is $1,015,664, and subtract the total expenses, which are $511,295. This gives us our NOI, which is $504,369.

Formula:

$$\text{Effective Gross Income} - \text{Total Expenses} = \text{NOI}$$
$$\$1,015,664 - \$511,295 = \$504,369$$

The capital reserves are what we pay into escrow every month, which is usually about $250-$300 per unit. We put this amount into the escrow account so that when a need arises, like roof replacements, air conditioning repairs, or anything like that, we have that money set aside. The NOI, after these capital expenses we anticipate in escrow, gives us a very important number - PRIMARY DEBT SERVICE. This is the number that really informs our mortgage potential.

ellers	Per Unit	% of GSR	Mortgage Info	
,003,494	$7,840		Purchase Price	$5,125,000
560,000	$469	6.0%	% Down	20%
511,193	$87	1.1%	Down Payment	$1,025,000
$0	$0	0.0%	Mortgage Amt	$4,100,000
$0	$0	0.0%	Interest Rate (ADD .25%)	4.75%
932,301	$7,284	92.9%	AM.Term (250yr if int. only)	30
$0	$0	0.0%	Annual Debt Service	$256,650
537,698	$295	3.8%	Interest Only Debt SVC (YR1)	$194,751
969,999	$7,578	96.7%	Closing/Acquisition Costs	
			Closing Costs	1.5%	$61,500
Sellers	Per Unit	% of GSR	Loan Points	1.0%
579,842	$624	8.0%	Loan Point Cost	$41,000
565,880	$515	6.6%	Acquisition Fee %	5.0%
558,873	$460	5.9%	Acquisition Fee Amount	$256,250
522,749	$178	2.3%	Legal Costs	$16,000
549,102	$384	4.9%	Total Closing Costs	$374,750

Total Closing Costs	$374,750
Capital Reserves	$38,400
1st Yr Insurance 100%	$42,000
Prop Tax Reserve (4 Mo)	$52,134
Utility Deposit	$15,000
Repair/ Maintenance Costs	$102,716
Total Acquisition Costs	$1,650,000

PLATE #3 – UNDERWRITING AND ANALYZING THE DEALS · 121

The purchase price is $5,125,000. The percentage we put down is 20%. We calculate the down payment, the mortgage amount, and the interest rate. It is necessary to add 0.25% to your mortgage interest rate during the underwriting process to account for the risk of an increase in your interest rate before you close on the property. The annual debt service at the end of this chart is what comes out in the chart above as the <u>primary</u> <u>debt</u> <u>service</u>.

In the previous chart, there is no secondary debt. The cash flow before taxes is $209,318. The Cash-on-Cash return (COC) is calculated as the cash flow from the previous chart, divided by total acquisition cost in the chart, which is $1,650,000.

Formula:

Cash Flow Before Taxes ÷ Total Acquisition Costs = Cash on Cash (COC)

$209,318 ÷ $1,650,000 = 12.7%

Keep in mind that the closing and the acquisition costs will be 1.5% - 2%. Usually, the syndicators get 3% - 5% of an acquisition fee. This is a good emerging market. Five percent acquisition fee was taken (in this example) to come up with the amount of $256,250. The total closing cost is also present. The capital reserves are what the lenders want to be given to them at the time of escrow closing, the capital reserves for one year.

Many lenders require that you pay the full insurance for the whole year upfront, as well as property tax reserves for four months and any utility deposits (utility companies may require a deposit from a new owner of the property). Maintenance costs are also present. The total acquisition cost is pulled from investors. The syndicators get all the money from the investors and it will show up in the PPM. We also take notes on some of the key factors regarding these anticipated incomes and expenditures.

Things to Consider

The Property

- Are the units individually metered?
- Is there a high demand for apartments?
- Is there a low vacancy rate for the property?

The Location

- Is your market growing?
- Are there any major employers in the area?
- Are the major industries in your area hiring?

We take notes about all the properties. Are the units individually metered? Is there a waiting list for tenants that can be provided by the manager? Take note of the $20,000,000 expansion rate in the next 40 years, indicating big area growths. All of the units are occupied even though we estimated an 8% vacancy rate, and they still have a waiting list. This is a good area.

PLATE #3 – UNDERWRITING AND ANALYZING THE DEALS · 123

Cash on Cash Return (COC)

Utility		$75,000	$586
Contract Services		$35,000	$250
Payroll		$134,400	$1,050
Total Expenses		$511,295	$3,994
Net Operating Income (NOI)		$504,369	
Capital Reserves	$300	$38,400	
NOI - After Capital Exp		$465,969	
Primary Debt Service		$256,650	
Secondary Debt Service		$0	
Cash Flow Before Taxes		$209,318	
Cash on Cash Return		12.7%	>12.4%
Debt Coverage Ratio		1.82	>1.6
Cap Rate (Including Capital Exp)		9.1%	>7.75
Managers Cash Flow		$83,727	40%
Equity Partners Cash Flow		$125,591	60%
COC Return Equity Partners		8.36%	
Debt Value (NOI/Debt)		12.3%	>10%

The COC of 12.7% and the debt coverage ratio of 1.82% indicates that the CAP rate, including the capital expenditure that we took out, is 9.1%. This is very exciting. Usually, we look for a COC of about 12% and a debt coverage ratio greater than 1.2. The CAP rate in the A area is usually about 7.75.

Cap Rate (Including Capital Exp)	9.1%	>7.75
Managers Cash Flow	$83,727	40%
Equity Partners Cash Flow	$125,591	60%
COC Return Equity Partners	8.36%	
Debt Value (NOI/Debt)	12.3%	>10%

Above, you will see the split of the cash flow. Here we are collecting 40%, which is $83,727. We divide that by the amount the equity partners are collecting, $125,591, and the COC return of the equity partners is 8.36% just in the first year alone. That is a lot of money for the first year. As we continue, we will look at how to project this return of 8.36% into another segment, yielding a projection of the next five years and so on.

COC represents the return on your cash investment after debt service.

Let's break down, now, all of these various parts of the cash on cash return. It will provide us a clearer picture, piece by piece, of the cash flow of the property.

Cash Flow = NOI – Debt Service – Cap Ex
Cash Flow/Cash Investment (Acquisition Cost)

In the cash flow, you have to take out the mortgage (debt service), which is the principal in the interest of the fixed interest-only loan. Sometimes, you are able to get one or two years of an interest-only loan, which is great if the lender allows it on the quality of the asset. This will mean that you are keeping the profit for the cash flow, etc., for renovations for the first couple of years. Most loans, though, are principal and interest loans, and if you take that out from the NOI, you are still left with money there. We also have something called Capex., which means capital reserve that is set aside for future repairs and improvements. Especially in multi-family, this is very common.

It is common to set aside $250-$300/unit/year for Cap Ex.

If you have a 100-unit complex, you need to set aside about $250-$300 per unit for the "rainy day" expenses. If the roof needs to be changed in five years or we need to buy appliances or put some upgrades to the landscapes or make other improvements, there must be money set aside. That money or Capex. is then taken out from the NOI. We take out the debt service minus the Capex., and that is your cash flow.

PLATE #3 – UNDERWRITING AND ANALYZING THE DEALS · 125

Capitalization Rate (CAP Rate)

The CAP rate is the rate of return on the investment. This metric provides a good indication of the yield of the property. One way to think about it is that it allows you to measure the rate of return on the property (excluding the debt service payment). CAP rates are used as a way to compare properties with similar characteristics to understand your risk-adjusted return. You should not expect to see the same CAP rates in Detroit, Michigan as you would find in San Francisco, California.

CAP Rate = NOI/Purchase Price

The Debt Service (mortgage) is not considered in the CAP Rate.

The CAP rate does not include "debt service." In talking about the deal, I never mention mortgage or debt service because in the CAP rate we do not include that. The CAP rate is always represented as a percentage number. For example, if the property is at 6% CAP, 8% CAP or 11% CAP, we are speaking of percentages. This is a Measurement of profitability as an asset with no respect for financing or leverage because, when we are buying a building, we are taking out a loan. For example, we might take a 70% loan with 30% down or an 80% loan with 20% down or split the difference with a 75% loan with 25% down. Regardless, the debt service is not counted in the CAP rate.

CAP rates are relative to each neighborhood and vary from area to area.

It is usual to compare the market or other similar properties to the CAP rate because it is in the same neighborhood. The CAP rates are also distinguished by the neighborhood. There could be lower CAP rates in the luxury areas but there might be a higher CAP rate by one to three percentage points if you move to the other side of that town. The lower the CAP rate, the higher the value of the asset. The higher the CAP rate, the lower the value of the asset.

Example:

Purchase Price $5,500,000
NOI   552,000

552,000/5,500,000 = 10% (CAP Rate)

For example, let's say you buy as an asset for $5,500,000, and then you find out the annual NOI that the seller is providing, according to their books, you also have to write their numbers down. However, you have to look at your numbers, too. If the NOI is $552,000, you divide the NOI by the $5,500,000. That number is the CAP rate. That CAP rate does not include debt service. It is not a number. It is, instead, a measure of the profitability as an asset with no respect for financing or leverage. It is a very useful figure to use in comparing with other markets and other similar properties.

Acquisition Cost

- Down Payment
- Closing Costs
- Loan Term Sheet (Origination Fee 1% + Other Fees)
- Legal Fees
- Escrow
- Acquisition Fee

Acquisition cost is the out of pocket expenses that we pay upfront to purchase the asset. The acquisition cost includes the down payment, closing costs, loan term sheets, and (sometimes) the origination fee or extra fees. In addition, some legal fees are involved. There are some escrows involved for the utility, insurance, and Capex.

The bank will require that you have expenditure reserves (typically $250-300/unit) kept in escrow (3-6 months) at the time of closing on the deal.

PLATE #3 – UNDERWRITING AND ANALYZING THE DEALS · 127

The lenders require some money to be kept in escrow at the time of the closing. The lender, therefore, keeps it on reserve for us, for the property to make sure we are not defaulting on it. They typically like to keep three to six months of reserves. All that money put together, along with the acquisition fee is called the acquisition cost.

When presenting investors with an opportunity, you are entitled to getting an Acquisition Fee for your efforts in putting the deal together.

Therefore, COC return is the cash flow divided by acquisition cost. This number is also represented as a percentage. It is also called Return on Investment (ROI). It is a measure of return on investment including financing or leverage. The difference between CAP rate and COC is that the leverage is covered in COC, the cash flow. It is useful to compare this figure to the ROI of further investments. If you look at the ROI of several properties, you want to determine the ROI or the COC to compare the properties, which, in turn, will give us more COC investment. Ultimately, we will be investing some or all of that acquisition cost to buy the next asset.

Example:

Purchase Price	$5,500,000
Acquisition Cost (32%)	1,800,000
Annual Cash Flow	216,000

216,000/1,800,000 = 12% COC

The next step I like to discuss talk about is the COC example (above). If the seller is selling a property at $5,500,000, and we need 32% to acquire it, we have to get $1,800,000 including the down payment, closing costs, legal fees, acquisition fee, and other fees. In other words, we need $1,800,000 in cash to buy the property. The annual cash flow is about $216,000. When we calculate the COC, it will be the cash flow, divided by the total amount that you are investing into that property. The resulting 12% is the COC return.

Annual Operating Assumptions

Annual Operating Assumptions						
	Year 1	Year 2	Year 3	Year 4	Year 5	Basis for Estimate
Rent Growth	1.0%	5.0%	5.0%	3.5%	3.0%	
[Per month]		$35	$37	$27	$24	[calculated per month increase]
Vacancy	6.0%	6.0%	6.0%	6.0%	6.0%	Avg Occ. = 93.9%
Concessions	1.0%	1.0%	1.0%	1.0%	1.0%	(Houston Sub Mkt for 8 prop)
Loss to Lease	1.5%	2.0%	1.5%	1.5%	1.5%	
Non-Revenue Units	0.0%	0.0%	0.0%	0.0%	0.0%	
Utility Reimb/dr/mo	$10	$10	$5	$3	$3	
Potentail Util Recapture	$15,360	$30,720	$38,400	$43,008	$47,616	
Percent Util Recapture (%)	20.5%	39.8%	48.3%	52.5%	56.4%	

In continuation of developing the property brochure for syndication and making sure that the investors like what you are offering as the syndicator, it is necessary to make some annual operating assumptions. In other words, how will the rent be growing? In the first year, when you buy the property, will it be 0% or 1% rental income growth? In the second year, when you take over the property, what will the growth be? You have to set assumptions of the projections of the income growth. You have to make assumptions even up to four or five years. Our syndication goal is we like to get into the emerging market and sell the asset.

A lot of our syndicators and lawyers have shared with us that you should consider a 5-7 year holding period when presenting the deal to investors because the investors' money is tied up in the asset, and they cannot liquidate it any sooner than that. Therefore, it is good to give a broader horizon, well beyond the two years. Whatever we write into the PPM (private placement memorandum) or the operating agreement, we want to make sure that we give enough time for the property to stabilize in value with the increasing of the rent and the decreasing of the expenses. The annual assumptions are very important, including the vacancy rate when purchasing the property, its fluctuation or consistency for that five to seven-year period.

We look at five-year projections in the brochures that we send to the investors. We address issues like what kind of concession the property

PLATE #3 – UNDERWRITING AND ANALYZING THE DEALS · 129

is giving. Likewise, loss of lease is a very important term, which means the difference between the potential rent of a unit and the actual rent received from that unit.

For instance, there is a market rental rate, but some of the tenants are not paying the rental rate because they have been there for a few years, and they are good tenants, so their rates are lower. It is very important to see what the loss of lease is, though. We should assume that it will stay at 1.5% or 2%. The non-revenue units are different. These units do not generate any actual rental income but serve a specific purpose. Maybe one is given up becoming a maintenance unit or one has been converted into an office.

Utility reimbursement is another assumption about which to speculate. Is the tenant paying all the utilities? Are the units metered individually? Are there utilities that we may be able to bill back to the client, such as electricity, water, garbage and sewer fees. If it is individually metered for electricity, the tenants will pay for that. The bill back system is simply another term for expense reimbursement. The main thing we want to see is that these assumptions are well taken care of before we go into our five-year pro forma and budget brochure that will be given to the investors.

5 Year Pro Forma and Budget							
		Year 1	Year 2	Year 3	Year 4	Year 5	
Revenues							
Gross Scheduled Rents (GSR)		$1,075,200	$1,128,960	$1,185,408	$1,226,897	$1,263,704	Enter annual increase in Table to Right>>
Vacancy (Avg)	6.0%	$64,512	$67,738	$71,124	$73,614	$75,822	Enter annual increase in Table to Right>>
Concessions		$10,752	$11,290	$11,854	$12,269	$12,637	Enter annual increase in Table to Right>>
Loss to Lease		16128	$22,579.2	17781.12	18403.4592	18956.583	Enter annual increase in Table to Right>>
Non-Revenue Units		0	0	0	0	0	Enter annual increase in Table to Right>>
Rental Income		$983,808	$1,027,354	$1,084,648	$1,122,611	$1,156,289	
Utility Reimbursement		$15,360	$30,720	$38,400	$43,008	$47,616	Enter annual increase in Table to Right>>
Other Income		$38,000	$39,140	$40,314	$41,524	$42,769	Increase Per Yr	3%
Total Income		$1,037,168	$1,097,214	$1,163,363	$1,207,143	$1,246,675	
Expenses							
Taxes at Rate of	2.543141%	$104,269	$106,354	$108,481	$110,651	$112,864	Increase Per Yr	2%
Insurance		$42,000	$42,000	$42,000	$42,000	$42,000	Note. Year1 Ins Amt less 1st Year of Insura
Repairs/Maintenance		$54,400	$56,032	$57,713	$59,444	$61,228	Increase Per Yr	3%
General/Administration		$16,000	$16,480	$16,974	$17,484	$18,008	Increase Per Yr	3%
Management	4.00%	$41,487	$43,889	$46,535	$48,286	$49,867	
Electric/Utility		$75,000	$77,250	$79,568	$81,955	$84,413	Increase Per Yr	3%
Marketing		$9,600	$9,888	$10,185	$10,490	$10,805	Increase Per Yr	3%
Contract Services		$36,000	$36,050	$37,132	$38,245	$39,393	Increase Per Yr	3%
Payroll		$134,400	$138,432	$142,585	$146,863	$151,268	Increase Per Yr	3%

Total Expenses		$512,156	$526,375	$541,172	$555,417	$569,846		
Expenses as ratio of Total Income		49%	48%	47%	46%	46%		
Net Operating Income (NOI)		$525,012	$570,838	$622,191	$651,725	$676,829		
Capital Reserves per door	$300	$38,400	$38,400	$38,400	$38,400	$38,400		
Cash Flow After Cap. Reserves		$486,612	$532,438	$583,791	$613,325	$638,429		
Debt Service @	4.75%	$256,650	$256,650	$256,650	$256,650	$256,650		IRR Calculation
Total Cash Flow After Debt Service		$229,962	$275,788	$327,141	$356,675	$381,779		Initial
		Year 1	Year 2	Year 3	Year 4	Year 5		Yr 1
Percent Distributions to Investors		60%	60%	60%	60%	60%		<<NOTE: ENTER CARV
Managers Cash Flow		$91,985	$110,315	$130,856	$142,670	$152,711	Cash Flow	Yr 2
Investor Cash Flow		$137,977	$165,473	$196,284	$214,005	$229,067	$942,806	Yr 3
Initial Equity Contribution		$1,650,000						Yr 4
							Total	Yr 5 ++
Investors Cash Flow Return								

This worksheet contains gross scheduled rent, which is increased in the second year following the assumptions that we made for the rent growth. We can also see the vacancies, concessions, loss of lease, and non-revenue units, as well as the rental income, utility reimbursements, and other income over the period of 1-5 years.

In looking at to the expenses, the biggest expense is usually tax rate. You have to figure out the exact percentage. It is called MIL RATE, and it is determined by the county. Check the MIL Rate in the area where you are buying the property. You can use companies that specialize in "contesting tax assessments," and they may be able to reduce your property tax. These are great services because they save you money as the years go on, but you should include the current MILL Rate in your projections rather than assuming you can find exceptions or exemptions. Better to be safe than sorry. You can see that the insurance, repairs, maintenance, general administration, management, electricity and utilities, marketing, contract services, and payroll are also present in the list of expenses.

Once total expenses are calculated, we can project the expenses for the ratio of total income. It is safe to assume that expenses will run less than 50% of your gross revenue. NOI (Net Operating Income) is the difference of the two values. The NOI should increase every year. In five years when you are selling the asset, the CAP rate at that time will determine the value of the property.

PLATE #3 – UNDERWRITING AND ANALYZING THE DEALS · 131

Forced Appreciation Factors

The rents will increase because of the following factors

- Inflation
- Growth in your market
- Shortage of Supply

Forced appreciation occurs when the rents are increased and when there is market inflation when the REA is getting better, and when there are fewer available apartments around. Beyond the forced appreciation of your property, you can increase its value and the rental incomes simply by putting value into it with upgrades and renovations.

Looking back to the chart, you can see the capital reserves per door, cash flow after CAP reserves, and removal of the mortgage (or debt service as it is called in commercial terms), and we are left with the total cash flow.

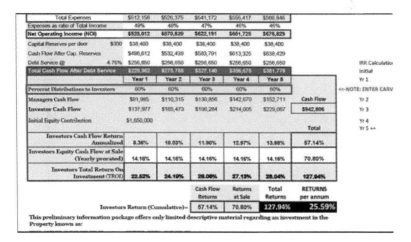

Percentage Distributions to the Investors

As the syndicator, you give about 60% to 70% of the total cash flow of the property to the investors, depending on the deal. Manager's cash flow is about 40%, and it is given to the manager. Initial equity contribution is where we calculate how much we raised to buy the property. We are able to calculate the "investors cash flow return (annualized)."

Formula:

$$\frac{Investor\ Cash\ Flow}{Initial\ Equity\ Contribution} = Investor\ Cash\ Flow\ Return$$

In this example, $\frac{\$137,977}{\$1,650,000} = 8.36\%$

This figure usually increases as the years go on. The total amount for all the years will also be calculated. When we sell the property, we have to calculate the CAP rate and figure out how much the proceeds will be at the end of five years. This depends on how quickly the emerging market is moving.

In this case, it is called the equity return at resale. We design the worksheet in our brochure, and it usually includes only the fifth year in the PPM. However, you can design it for a period of 2-5 years to show the investors. The NOI is present in this worksheet. We also calculate the exit price at the end of the year. We project the CAP rate - will it remain the same as when you bought it, or will it be decreasing? If the CAP rate decreases, it means the market is getting better and the properties will be worth more. The future sales prices and CAP rate are based on your assumptions of where the market will be. Be conservative in your assumptions. We usually write CAP rate as remaining the same as when we bought it.

You will want to take out the sales expenses, closing costs, and initial loan principal, which is what is used to pay the mortgage back. In the worksheet, the principal pay-down is present because we are going to pay interest for all these years. The owner equity, less initial investment, is also calculated. The equity created is the owner equity minus the less initial investment. The manager's share of equity and the investor's net equity share is calculated. You divide the investor's net equity share by the number of years to determine what the investors' net equity growth

PLATE #3 – UNDERWRITING AND ANALYZING THE DEALS · 133

will be percentage-wise and annualized. We then put that back into our five-year projection. That number is added to the investors' cash flow per year, and the total is the investors' total return, which is annualized. It is called TROI (total return of investors).

Equity Return At Resale		2nd Year	3rd Year	4th Year	5th year
NOI at the end of year		$570,839	$622,191	$651,725	$676,829
Exit Price at end of _ year at CAP	8.75%	$6,523,873	$7,110,732	$7,448,291	$7,733,186
Sales Expense	4%	($260,955)	($284,430)	($297,932)	($309,407)
Closing Costs	1%	($65,239)	($71,108)	($74,483)	($77,332)
Initial Loan Principal		($4,100,000)	($4,100,000)	($4,100,000)	($4,100,000)
Principal Pay down		$229,604	$299,760	$372,097	$348,572
Owner Equity		$2,227,283	$2,854,376	$3,247,973	$3,596,999
Less Initial Investment		($1,650,000)	($1,650,000)	($1,650,000)	($1,650,000)
Equity Created		$577,283	$1,204,376	$1,597,972	$1,946,998
Manager's share of equity (Y12-5) -> 40%		$230,913	$481,750	$639,189	$778,799
Investor's Net Equity Share (Yr 2-5)-> 60%		$346,370	$722,626	$958,783	$1,168,199
Investor's Net Equity % (Cumulative)		20.99%	43.80%	58.11%	70.80%
Investor's Net Equity Growth (Annualized)		10.5%	14.6%	14.5%	14.16%
Investor's Cash Flow Return (Annualized)		10.0%	11.0%	12.0%	13.0%
Investor's Return (Cumulative) After _ Years		39.4%	74.1%	101.4%	127.9%
Investor's Total Return (Annualized)		19.7%	24.7%	25.3%	25.6%

In the previous chart, the total of the TROI shows investors the cash flow and the acuity together. These make up the investors' cumulative return. These are great numbers providing valuable information what will result in everybody wanting to invest with you.

Purchase Price		$5,125,000
Less Loan Amount		$4,100,000
Down payment Equity		$1,025,000
Approximate Closing Costs:		
Syndication fee & Other Legal		$16,000
Real Estate Lawyer fee		$2,500
Loan Origination Fee	1.0%	$41,000
Lender fees/ Survey/ Appraisal		$16,000
Loan Processing Fee		$7,500
Lender Escrows		$2,600
3rd Party Reports		$11,500
Misc. Other		$18,000
Organization and Due Diligence (Acquisition Fee)		$256,250
Total Closing Costs =		$371,350
Capital Improvement Reserve		$38,400
1st Year Insurance Premium		$42,000
Utility Deposit		$15,000
Property Tax Reserves-FNMA (6 mo)		$52,134
Repair/ Maintenance Costs		$106,116
Cash Requirements @ Closing/ Member Equity		$1,650,000

Note: Closing costs are estimates and will be finalized upon
acceptance and commitment of loan package.

This takes us to the part of the brochure we will show to the investors. It deals primarily with how much we are going to be collecting. We also show how this money will be used. Using this as an example, the first thing we write is the purchase price. We pay this amount to the seller. Less loan amount and down payment, equity is written into this part of the brochure. We analyze the approximate closing costs that we will expect in this transaction. The syndication fee and other legal fees take a significant amount of money. For this reason, it is important to work with a qualified syndication attorney for preparing the PPM and investment package.

If you do not have a good lawyer, I can recommend some qualified syndicate attorneys to you. A Syndication attorney is separate from your real estate attorney. The real estate lawyer fee is included in the costs. They look through LLCs and compose the letter of intent (LOI). Real estate lawyers help to take care of many details pertaining to closing the deal. Because each deal is different, you cannot just copy an existing PPM. This is one of the places a syndication attorney becomes essential

PLATE #3 – UNDERWRITING AND ANALYZING THE DEALS · 135

- to write your PPM. Lawyers are expensive but do not worry about the cost because it is the investors who raise money for this expense. In the long run, you will save yourself a lot of money and time by having a great lawyer.

Loan origination fee is about 1%. Lender fees, surveys, and appraisals are included. Surveys and appraisals, by the way, are from third parties, so their fees could be more expensive. Loan processing fees are also present. Lenders escrows are important because, as we have explained, the lenders require that you place a portion of the capital reserves in an escrow account.

The lenders will keep the escrow for the capital improvement reserve, the first-year insurance premium, utility deposits, property tax reserves, and repair/maintenance costs. Another significant expense is the organization and due diligence (acquisition fee, but the IRS requires us to use the *organization and due diligence fee* as the term). The typical acquisition fee ranges from 1% to 5% of the sale price.

All of these costs are calculated and the total is the cash required at closing. It also includes the member equity. Remember to put into the brochure a disclosure that reads, "NOTE: Closing costs are estimates and will be finalized upon acceptance of and commitment to loan package."

These are all important parts of the brochure we put together for the investors. Let these costs be known to the investors. You must keep your investors well informed and provide full disclosure of everything! As a syndicator, you have to abide by the SEC laws. This is the way to survive and make sure you are reaching your goal and dreams, as well as those of the other stakeholders in the deal.

What's in It for Me?

Before we leave this plate spinning and move on to Plate #4, it is important that we discuss the great advantages and benefits experienced by the syndicator (YOU) in the deals. These are rules of thumb or estimated numbers and percentages only. Again, each deal is unique, but this will provide a good indication of what you can expect.

The syndicator can be paid for four different events in the life cycle of the deal.

1. Acquisition
2. Operations
3. Refinance
4. Sale of the property

Syndicators typically earn between 25% and 60% of distributable cash generated from operations, refinance, or sale of a property, which may be paid as a direct split between the members and the syndicator (i.e., 65/35) or as a preferred return.

Fees are an expense of the syndication and may be collected by the syndicator on a monthly, quarterly, or annual basis. The types of fees a syndicator may earn are:

1. Acquisition fee (1% to 4% of the purchase price)

2. Asset management fee (1% to 2% of gross collected revenue)

3. Refinance fee (1% to 2% of the refinance loan amount)

4. Disposition fee (1% to 3% of the sale price)

5. Loan guarantor fee (1% to 3% of the loan amount or a flat fee)

6. Interest on loans made to the company (8% to 12% of the loan amount)

PLATE #3 – UNDERWRITING AND ANALYZING THE DEALS · 137

Real Estate Brokerage Fees. A syndicator who is a licensed real estate broker or agent in the state where the property is located may also earn commissions or fees for providing licensed brokerage activities to the syndication, including:

1. Commissions on purchase of the property need to be included in the PPM

2. Resale commissions need to be included in the PPM

3. Property management fees (3% to 7%, the lower the number of units the higher the fee)

Expense Reimbursement. In addition to the fees and distributions a syndicator may earn, the syndicator can be reimbursed for payments he or she makes to third parties during the organization of the company, due diligence/acquisition, or operation of the property.

In my case, we formed our own Management Companies and managed 100% of the assets through the whole life cycle right up until disposition. We have completed 10 as of this writing and have another 4 nearing their terms as specified in the PPM and Operating Agreements.

Syndication is exciting! It is especially exciting when the investors are getting the types of returns we have discussed in this chapter. They can open up more wallets, and you can uncover money that you did not know they had. They will be happy to be all in because they do not have to do all the work but can trust you to safeguard their money. Syndication has risks, and all investors should know that, but when the returns you are giving back to the investors are strong, they will invest and tell other people about it who may invest, too.

CHAPTER SIX

Plate #4 – Loan Qualification (The Big Elephant)

It occurs to me that we can be spinning the first three plates with minimal attention drawn to ourselves, but this fourth plate is when we really draw the eye of an audience - most often the bankers! Nevertheless, **loan qualification** is one of the many responsibilities of the syndicator, so we must address Plate #4. Let's be honest, the idea of sitting before a loan officer with all of your financials exposed is about as enticing as that annual physical examination at the doctor's office with...well, everything exposed. There is good news, though. Obtaining loan qualification for a multi-family syndication deal is not that bad.

In fact, compared to a personal loan, it is a fairly painless process. It is actually easier to get a loan for a multifamily home than a single-family home. Although it takes more money to finance a multifamily property, loan lenders prefer lending for this kind of property. In fact, they would rather lend money on a 100-unit apartment complex than for a single unit building or single-family home. This is because the banks believe in the security that comes along with investing in a stabilized apartment complex & they have so much money that it takes them (the banks) much less risk & much fewer transactions to grow it at a good rate.

In this chapter, we will discuss how to finance your first deal and how to get your first loan. For me, when we first started, it was quite difficult to get that first loan. It definitely takes being persistent, dreaming big, and standing tall. My partner and I started with our passion, drive, positive attitude, and $500. We were eager to take on a commercial real estate deal, so we were busy analyzing several of them and learning what we could about them from universities and coaching programs. Through all of our daily education and implementation, it still took us almost ten months to close our first deal.

Friends and Family/Personal Investors

Our first financing came not from a bank but from a relative who was able to give us a small loan. You can start with a little capital, with a very limited real estate background, and you can move forward. Though the small loan from a relative or friend is an option for those starting out, it is important to have a plan for financing that goes beyond that first deal. Banks typically have deeper pockets than relatives, so we want to try to go that route as soon as we can.

Be warned! If you mix your business with family, you are exposing both of them to danger. You will not enjoy family gatherings that are turned into arguments over loan repayment and other related issues. If you are convinced your relationship will not be adversely affected, go ahead with it. Some people have used this type of loan to launch a successful business. A note of caution though – it is important that everybody involved in the business should sign a promissory note to serve as collateral against repayment problems if they arise. As financial expert Dave Ramsey says, **"Thanksgiving dinner tastes 100% better** when friends or relatives don't owe one another money" ("The Danger Zone")!

Securing finances for our first few deals was a major hurdle. Starting out in 2008, the housing collapse caused many banks and individuals to

PLATE #4 – LOAN QUALIFICATION (THE BIG ELEPHANT) · 141

keep a tight fist on their cash. The stock market was fluctuating. Fore-
closures were happening everywhere. Many banks around the country
were really tightening their lending requirements. Consequently, they
were not lending money for commercial real estate. Fortunately for us,
they were lending for multi-family real estate, which was quickly becoming our expertise. In our minds, we were at low risk and had secure,
well-paying jobs. We were dabbling in real estate part-time. We thought
our business plan was strong. We had good credit. The bankers, however, did not see it the way we did.

See, the lenders asked questions like, "What kind of experience you
have? What properties do you own? Lenders always want to look into
or are interested in your record of accomplishments. We were able to
convince the bank that, though we were just starting up, we had looked
into these properties and had formulated a detailed plan of attack. That
was how we got our first deal. When applying for your first loan, convince the banks that you are passionate and well prepared to invest in
real estate. Give them the assurance that their money is secure with you.

Banks still prefer lending for the financing of multifamily property, and
after all we have discussed so far, you can probably guess why. For one
thing, multifamily property guarantees steady cash flow far more reliable than single-family units. Think about it: if the tenant of a single-
family property leaves, the home becomes 100% vacant, which is bad
for business. If a tenant of a 10-unit multifamily property leaves the
property, the vacancy is only 10%, leaving 90% of the property as a
source of income until the vacant apartment is rented again. This ensures steady cash flow for the property owner and reduces the
probability of a foreclosure, which is a very valid reason for lenders to
be willing to give the loan, as they consider it a less risky investment in
comparison the owner of a single-family property.

Bank Loans

A bank loan is considered by many aspiring entrepreneurs as the preferred way out of a cash crunch when capital is not readily available to finance their business deals. Before a bank will give you a loan, the bank will request a detailed business plan to give them insight into your business and its prospects. The bank will also want a business proposal that will communicate the product or service you are offering. They (the bankers) will ask for the management and financial projections, as well as your process by which you will turn your plans into reality. This is all to assure the bank that you have a feasible business that is worth its investment. Without a good business plan and proposal, a bank will surely refuse your loan application.

The easiest way to obtain the financing you seek from a bank is to approach a bank with which you already have a good relationship. This will give you an edge and increase your chances of getting the loan far more than if you were to contact a bank where you are relatively unknown. Remember, banks are out to make money too. So, they will want to invest in a business idea that guarantees a good return on investment for their money.

Let's dig in!

Steps for Getting Financing

Here are some of the steps that you might want to consider as you seek to get financing.

Step 1: Build relationships with a few loan brokers

I recommend that you build strong relationships with some loan brokers because they are the people who can open up the horizon for you. It is the business of loan brokers to find out what is out there, what kind of

PLATE #4 – LOAN QUALIFICATION (THE BIG ELEPHANT) · 143

loans are available in the area where you are purchasing commercial property. They will charge 1% as an origination fee, which is the same as most banks or direct lenders. When using a broker, you will not have to pay 2%, one percent to the brokers and one percent to the lenders. The one origination fee charged by the broker will be it.

When we started out, we first sought financing from the local community banks. We met with officials there and showed them our properties. These local banks gave us more of a hearing than the big banks did then. Your local community bank is a great place to start, and they will more than likely listen to your vision and give you a loan.

Step 2: Build relationships with local community banks

One of the key components to a deal that lenders really care about is the "skin in the game." The lenders have asked us each time, "How much are you guys bringing into the deal?" Lenders are interested in the amount you are putting in. But, to be honest, we never put any money into the deal. Well, we did put $1,000 in to control the interest of our equity and cash flow. That is how our syndication lawyers have always designed it. So, keep in mind that it is not necessary that you have "skin in the game." You can use your investors' *skin.* With that said, by putting some of your own capital in, you will boost the confidence of the lenders toward you. When you are willing to risk your money, the lenders see it differently.

Step 3: Prepare for having some 'skin in the game'
    – Be prepared for a personal guarantee

When going to the lenders, you must present the whole deal with specifics. Show lenders the business plan for your deal. Be prepared for personal guarantees. The lenders typically demand that you place a personal guarantee in the deal.

Step 4: Bring a loan sponsor in the deal (as a partner)

You can bring a partner in as a loan sponsor. The loan sponsor typically receives cash flow and equity shares in the deal so that they can qualify as one of the borrowers on that first loan with you. Often times the banks will want to see liquidity equal to six months of mortgage payments and a net worth equal to the loan balance. While searching for a partner to bring in for purposes of a loan, their experience is not as important as their net worth and liquidity.

Confidence goes a long way in the lending business, so be confident! You need to display your self-assurance to show your strengths as you dialogue with the loan brokers, bankers, and others. Your presentation should be professional and thorough. You might not have a lot of experience, so, as they say, "fake it 'til you make it!" After a few attempts, whether successful or not, you have learned what questions to ask. And now that you know them, write down the answers so that you can be confident and clear and erase any doubts about your inexperience.

Look professional. Follow up with lenders and loan brokers. This may seem unnecessary, but the lenders consider everything before they extend their loans to you. They are giving you a sizeable sum of money, and you need to assure them that this money is not wasted.

Seller Financing

Another option other than a loan is seller financing. To accomplish your first deal, you might want to look into seller financing. For this option, you should look at some commercial assets where the seller might be willing to finance the deal, though they might not advertise that fact. Ask the brokers and the sellers. This was really helpful for us when nobody wanted to give us a loan. Lenders are looking for experience, so seller financing is a great way to circumvent that requirement and

PLATE #4 – LOAN QUALIFICATION (THE BIG ELEPHANT) · 145

get a loan. If this is the route you take, be triumphant over it, for with these first few properties you are setting a trend.

Strive to succeed in your first few deals and build a strong record of accomplishment. Your ability to borrow in the future will be based on how well you have succeeded in getting a few properties under your belt. The experience helps, and the lenders might even keep asking you when you want to borrow more money. Every lender is different, and every borrower faces different obstacles. Do not give up! Keep trying until you get the loan you need. At all cost, work your first deal! Look into private money if you have to, which may come from family, friends, and hard-earned money of your own. Of course, there are pros and cons to every financing deal, so consider your choices carefully...but don't let anything stop you from conquering your first deal! Set a good trend! Keep on going!

At this point, you may be overwhelmed a little by the vast amount of work a syndicator must accomplish. Is it worth it? You were thinking that you would like to get into Multifamily Syndication to raise you and your family to a better and more comfortable lifestyle, all while helping others around you? Let me go ahead and relieve your worry by telling you that this model is 1000% worth it and share with you just how syndicators get paid. I have highlighted <u>six</u> different ways in which you will make money and achieve your financial goals.

For our investors to understand the preferred return percentage, the various other fees required, the investment selection, and the acquisition process we must go through to select just the "right" investment option for them, we present the following explanation:

1. Cash Flow Class A: You receive a preferred return of 8% per annum. Class B only gets a return once this is paid to Class A members. One-fourth of 8% is paid each of the first three quarters, and then for the fourth quarter, the balance of the 8% is paid, plus, if there is excess cash flow, an adjustment, and further payment. If the cash is insufficient, Class A members are paid what Class B would get until the 8% for the year is reached, and Class B's payments are deferred until there is sufficient cash.

2. Split between Investors and Management: In the first year, the investors receive 65% of the cash flow and the gain accruing (inherent, not realized) while the managers are compensated 35% of the cash flow and gain accruing. In years two through five, the investors receive 60% of the benefits, and the managers receive 40%. In most syndications, the range of compensation for the managers is 20% to 50%. In our syndications, it is typically 35% to 40%.

3. Property Management Fee of 4%: For a while in our organization, properties were managed by outside, third-party companies at the rate of 6% to 7% or higher. Management fees plus expenses were running very high for the return in the value we were realizing and quality of management we were experiencing. Therefore, about five years ago, I decided to start my own management company and find the best managers in the business. I sought those who had a minimum of 20 years of experience to work at the top of the company and others who had at least 10 years of experience to work at all other levels of the company.

Due to the fact that the property managers were now our employees, the asset management of each property could be assured of far better performance and tighter control of expenses. We set up this affiliate company to charge only 4% in management fees to cover its costs. Compared to typical management fees for multi-family properties of 6-10% (6% being more typical of larger numbers of units in Texas), and 8-10% for smaller properties, we were able to provide a significant savings for investors. One drawback of outside management companies is the tendency for them to run rampant with expense, but our new affiliate company eliminated that problem, as well. Property management fees

PLATE #4 – LOAN QUALIFICATION (THE BIG ELEPHANT) · 147

are always based on rents rather than on property equity, and, therefore, do not affect our investors' deal.

4. Due Diligence Fees of 2-4%: This is, admittedly, somewhat of a misnomer and is used as a miscellaneous category for all that the managers do to find and lock down a property. It is a one-time fee that really is not a fee at all but is, instead, compensation for all of the work performed in finding and offering a quality property. Let's discuss what the management company does in this process.

First, the managers have to study a geographic area on a continuing basis to determine the quality of the market, the job growth, the industry trends, and the investments by the state, county, and city agencies, all in an effort to ascertain if the market is still viable for upward growth— i.e., is it still an emerging market capable of providing us top quality results.

Secondly, the managers have to study the market for multi-family assets within that geographic area to determine if there are viable assets that may be coming on the market. It may take looking over financials for dozens of properties in order to find between six and ten properties that warrant a deeper dive and study.

Thirdly, the management company must continually meet and assess brokers to determine (1) who has the best sellers and assets, (2) the feasibility of negotiating a good deal, (3) who actually works regularly in the geographic market, and (4) the size and class of the market. Multi-family assets range from Class A properties in Class A neighborhoods down to Class D properties in Class D neighborhoods (these are referred to as Class "Don't!").

We often operate in Class B properties in Class B neighborhoods for one type of asset called "Momentum Plays" because the momentum of the market moves them up in value if there is job and industry growth and good management. We also work in Class C properties (or B-) in Class B neighborhoods. The latter is the type we can get under contract through astute negotiations with built-in equity by the time the ink is dry on the contract. These have great upside potential. Due to our management skills and excellent teams and contractor crews, we can turn these properties around just like a corporate turnaround expert does with larger corporations. We refer to these as "Value Plays."

Finding brokers who actually can bring deals is really a combination of art and science. It takes quite a bit of work to develop a relationship where the property does not even become a "pocket listing," and is exclusively offered to one buyer (you). I have learned to excel in this particular area.

Fourthly, we must assess, at a high level, the dozens of possible property deals and narrow it down to a list of six to ten, as stated above. Once that half dozen or so are identified, three or so are selected for a more in-depth analysis. In the final cut, one is chosen for the deep analysis and review of all the documents we can obtain from the broker and/or owner. This deeper analysis can take a long time between the broker, the owner, the records provided, a preliminary discussion with potential lenders, and other analyses that must be done far in advance of any LOI or offer.

As a fifth task, negotiations must occur between us (as a potential buyer) and the current owner. We must prepare an LOI, having analyzed all pertinent information available based on substantial underwriting spreadsheets designed with analytical guidelines. The LOI is then presented to the broker and the *dance* begins.

Sixth, we have discussions with some of our situated investors to determine if the property is interesting to them.

PLATE #4 – LOAN QUALIFICATION (THE BIG ELEPHANT) · 149

Seventh, if the LOI is signed by the owner, our RE attorney becomes involved in writing and finalizing the sales contract and wiring the earnest money ($50,000 to $100,000 usually) to the Escrow/Title company. There are then inspections and property due diligence to accomplish - some fun things like walking the property and "mystery shopping" it with our people. We must begin working with contractors of all types— roof, plumbing, HVAC, soil, structural, electrical, etc., to find out if this will be a viable deal.

Eighth, if the asset appears to be viable and still awaiting an actual decision, we must start the dialog with potential lenders to find the best deals out there at the moment. We must apply for and qualify for a loan for millions of dollars. You can imagine how detailed that is, and it relies very heavily, if not solely, on the syndicator's past record and his personal guarantee. He puts himself, his personal assets, and his company up for detailed scrutiny. It requires many meetings and conversations, as well as an imposing amount of paperwork.

The ninth step brings us to the work we need to do with our in-house (or outside, depending on your situation) property managers to determine how best to manage this potential property and to what extent any "re-managing" might need to be done.

Tenth, we need to do several site visits, walking the property and viewing the details of the asset, often getting rough bids and estimated costs of repairs and trying our best to negotiate a repair allowance that can be paid by the seller to the buyer (us) at closing.

Still progressing to the eleventh step, we need to begin investor relations materials, domain names, website input, preliminary brochures, and pro forma, as we develop the informational marketing materials for investors.

Twelfth, we work with two sets of attorneys: syndication lawyers, who obtain the SEC offering exemption and the Private Placement Memorandum (PPM), and business attorneys, who finalize the business structures and ownership packages and field any legal issues we may have.

Thirteenth, we hire independent professionals or professional companies to perform property surveys and appraisals and verify the owner's claims and disclosures regarding the property.

Fourteenth, we re-analyze, decide, and take upfront risks to execute a contract, knowing we will have to go hard with tens of thousands of dollars to secure the deal. "Go hard" refers to the point at which once you have the property under contract, and your deposit is no longer refundable. Often times, in the beginning, you want to structure your contracts, so nothing goes hard under after the 14-30 day due diligence period you negotiate.

Fifteenth, when the contractor and other inspections come in, we may have to re-negotiate for reductions or credits to the contract.

Sixteenth and finally! If for some reason, the deal does not go forward, we lose the money that has been placed down hard on the deal, perhaps tens of thousands of management company dollars, in addition to the money paid for all the due diligence inspections and the reports prepared (long before investor money has come in). This may amount to hundreds of thousands of dollars at risk by you or your investment group. This is why it is so important you do proper due diligence up front and negotiate the terms of your contract in accordance with your experience and risk tolerance.

Remember, this is just a recap of what the management company does long before investors are on the scene and for which our compensation is a one-time 4% of the purchase price. We understand that the term *Due Diligence* in the PPM is neither descriptive nor explanatory, and

PLATE #4 – LOAN QUALIFICATION (THE BIG ELEPHANT) · 151

we hope this explanation helps the investor understand what we do for our compensation. This amount pays expenses, wages and partner compensation if there is any net after expenses. While it is called a "Due Diligence" or "Acquisition" Fee, it encompasses far more than what we can put on a simple spreadsheet or in simple words in a FAQ list. It can take six or more months, thousands of phone calls and emails, meetings, and paperwork, and we still might lose thousands of dollars and end up with no asset. This is why we are paid that 4% "fee." We only get paid when we land a good property for our investors. We can all agree that the word "fee" is an inadequate term for compensation we receive for the services we provide, but that is the industry term for it, so we use it.

5. Split of Cash Flow: As stated above, when cash flow begins in the first year, the investors receive 65% of it, and the management LLC receives 35% of it. For the investor, that is a full 65%, with a preferred return of 8% -10% per annum *based on the actual dollar investment of the investor unreduced by fees or expenses*. For the management company, it is gross revenue subject to operating expenses before profit is made. In years two through five, the split is 60% to the investors and 40% to the management company. The preferred return still holds, but by this time the property is better managed and producing sufficient revenue.

6. Refinance/Sale Fee: If the net operating income (NOI) has increased sufficiently to raise the value of the property, the managers may decide the property can be refinanced. Each geographic area has a market CAP rate. NOI divided by CAP rate gives the value of the property. For example, if the property was purchased at $5 million and it produced $500,000 a year in NOI, the CAP rate would be 10%. That tells us the property has less value (poor management, low tenant quality, disrepair) than other properties in the area (there's an inverse ratio of CAP rate and value). If the NOI is increased over time through proper management, correcting the above mentioned problems, to $550,000 and the area's market CAP rate is 8%, the property is brought in line with other good quality properties, and its value will have increased to $6,875,000. This may warrant a refinance.

At this point, the managers must go through the same steps it took when first acquiring the property in locating a good lender, negotiating terms, working with attorneys, working with property managers, reviewing and executing documents, and finalizing a loan on good terms. This often results in a cash-out refi. For this work, the managers are paid a compensation of 1.5% of the loan amount, and the net proceeds are distributed to the investors by terms of the PPM and SEC rules. This "fee" is tantamount to a trustee performing duties other than regular daily operations of the entity, and an extra fee is allowed. That is the basis for this compensation—the managers have added on an extra job of reworking the financing.

At some point, it may be wise to sell the property and reinvest in another. At this point, the managers become sellers and must then find the best broker to negotiate the top price in the market. The managers must prepare, along with the broker, marketing materials and negotiate with buyers until one is found who is offering a good price. This will again require spreadsheets and analyses to determine when and for how much the property will be sold. This work is compensated at 1.5% of the sale price. This "fee" is again an extraordinary fee in that it is not management and operation on a daily basis but is a one-time, add-on job.

The equity split upon this sale follows the same percentage formula as the cash flow: 60% to investors and 40% to the management company. As you can see, the property is purchased with built-in gain (equity) at the outset due to wise negotiation. Therefore, the *fee* is actually inherent with this built-in gain and, at the final split, the investors' share of equity is not affected or reduced by those fees.

So, as you can see, this plate is one of the most important ones we will spin. However, it is also the one that is most likely to break apart the

PLATE #4 – LOAN QUALIFICATION (THE BIG ELEPHANT) · 153

entire deal if it is not spun well. Unless you have lots and lots of disposable money with which to finance your entire deal, loan qualification is a non-negotiable part of the multi-family syndication process. You work a lot harder spinning this fourth plate, but this is where you really begin to earn that extra money that is coming your way as the manager/syndicator of the deal. You can do it!!

CHAPTER SEVEN

Plate #5 – Asset Take Over and Property Management

I always like to say **the operation of the asset is much more important and difficult than the acquisition of it.** That operation or management of the asset begins on the day of closing when, all of a sudden, you are the proud owner of a 100 or 200 or 250-unit apartment home community. What now? This just became real!

It is imperative that we prepare ourselves fully for what must happen on the day of closing. The takeover process is detailed and must take place smoothly. Hopefully, you have decided to either self-manage the asset (which is what we do on all of our acquisitions) or you have hired a professional management company, and that company is on site and ready to begin serving you and your tenants.

What's next? To answer that question, let me share with you a document that we have put together over the years. It is our step-by-step checklist for asset takeover. I call it the **"Asset Take-Over Checklist!"**

TAKEOVER CHECKLIST – MONEIL MANAGEMENT GROUP
(Property Name)

PRIOR TO TAKEOVER (30 days)		Completed Date/Initials
Complete due diligence		
Evaluate current staff		
Complete Comparative Market Survey		
Place employment ads if necessary		
Create a wish list for capital improvements		
Interview Mgt./ Staff		
PRIOR TO TAKEOVER (10 DAYS-1 WEEK OUT)		
Schedule and order phone service –get pricing		
Order banner: new management, new attitude		
Order Computer, Scanner, Fax & Copier		
Schedule set-up property in RealPage		
Schedule set-up of rent roll		
Set up of initial rent schedule / match pro forma		
Set-up pagers - How Many?		
Set-up helium balloon account		
Set-up Vendor accounts (Home Depot/Lowes,)		
Make brochure /floor plans/		
Set-up landscape service account		
Set-up pest control service		
Set-up courtesy patrol		
Set-up alarm/monitoring system account (if applicable)		
Copy of personal inventory		
Set-up legal account for evictions/collections		
Set-up and get new bank account		

PLATE #5 – ASSET TAKE OVER AND PROPERTY MANAGEMENT · 157

DAY OF TAKEOVER		Completed Date/Initials
Copies of ON DATE OF TAKEOVER: 1. Current Rent Schedule 2. Security Deposit Report 3. Audit Prepaid Reports 4. Confirm delinquencies / copies of backup for files 5. Ledgers run on all units 6. Apartment Status Report 7. Receive copies of pending litigation 8. Utility bills and contract services bills (fax to Accounting to change services to new owner)		
Deliver resident takeover letters		
Contact locksmith and coordinate re-keying of office and safe combination		
Complete all new hire paperwork and overnight to HR		
Employees scheduled for screening Date scheduled:		
Review all approved applications		
Check and walk new move ins		
Walk all vacants, common areas		
Take 24 pictures the day of takeover		
Hang Rental Occupancy & Guidelines		
Hang Fair Housing Poster		
Set-up answering machine/voicemail service (change message) Completed on:		
Contact vendor to change hours on front door		
Rearrange employees' schedules based on new hours		
Confirm all utilities are transferred over -		

Pick model – Style: Apt #: Served:		
Order Maintenance Uniforms from Uniforms Inc.		
Initial office supply order – include disposable cameras		
Set-up rehab grid with current vacants		
Set-up projected occupancy reports and weekly numbers reports		
Manger, Assistant Manager, Bookkeeper and Leasing Agent –files set up		
Disposal of all old management forms / box misc. old mgmt info.		
Set-up computer system with property information		
WEEK TWO OF TAKEOVER		**Completed** **Date/Initials**
Set up ongoing ad online (Craig's List, Angie's List, etc.)		
Set up website		
Assess view premiums and create a new rent schedule for rental rates		
Contact vendors for accurate insurance / contracts		
Office Alarm System – Contact: Insurance:		
Pest Control Service – Contact: Insurance:		
Pool contract Service Contact: Insurance:		

PLATE #5 – ASSET TAKE OVER AND PROPERTY MANAGEMENT · 159

Courtesy Patrol – Contact: Insurance:		
Landscape Service – Contact: Insurance:		
Trash Contract – Contact: Insurance:		
Elevator Contract – Contact: Insurance:		
Vending Contract – Contact: Insurance:		
Laundry Contract – Contact: Insurance:		
Cable Contract – Contact: Insurance:		
Update Business License with city / post in office – Grant Deed and Closing Statement required –		
Complete typed copy of inventory		
Set-up before / after photo album		
Set-up budget in Software program		
Order final set-up business cards upon staff verifications		
WEEK THREE OF TAKEOVER		**Completed Date/Initials**
Set-up of Vendor Contract Book – Within 30 days:		
Set-up of MSDS Binder – within 30 days		
Complete takeover status summary		

Set-up demographics within 45 days:		
Rewalk common storage areas and mainte-nance shops		
Verify status of final brochures – Rec'd:		
Verify status of new ads – reviewed:		
WEEK FOUR OF TAKEOVER		
Renegotiate Laundry Contract –		
Renegotiate Cable Contract		
Purchase property name and logo mats –		
Contact local fire company to confirm signage / check fire extinguishers		
Send out lead/asbestos letter (if applicable) and confirm signed receipt,		
Send out 30-day notice of change of terms with new community rules and regulations / new late fee and amount		

As syndicators and investors plan the takeover of their new asset, a question that is on everyone's mind is "Do property management companies always try to raise rents on the properties they operate?"

It is a very good question. Before answering it, though, for your new property, it is important to have a good understanding of the rental market that your property resides in. You need to investigate the market where the property is located. In order to do this conduct a market rent study. A market rent study is done by the community manager or leasing agent by going out to the other, similar properties nearby and then tabulating certain statistics into a spreadsheet.

Shopping properties to see their grounds and staff is a great practice as well, as you can see your competition to evaluate their weaknesses and strengths. The study should include:

PLATE #5 – ASSET TAKE OVER AND PROPERTY MANAGEMENT · 161

- Property name
- Number of units located within that property
- The vintage
- Rental rate for one, two, three bedroom, etc.
- Amount of administrative Fee
- Amount of concessions
- Amount charged for utilities, etc.
- Occupancy rate
- Special rates

These types of studies should be conducted monthly. In fact, sometimes it is helpful to compile this data as often as weekly or bi-weekly. By doing so from time to time, you will truly be able to see what the competition within your market is offering. So these studies must be done monthly to keep tabs on the neighboring properties. Sometimes, I even ask our managers to do it by weekly every two weeks because that way you'll really know what the competition is about.

Those statistics then determine if you can increase rent or not. It is entirely based on the market; the demand and the occupancy level. The occupancy level will tell you whether the other properties are 93% occupied or 89% or 97%. You need to compare that occupancy level to your own. As a rule of thumb, if your property is 100% occupied (or even 99%) occupied, you can assume that your rents are low for that market.

Multifamily, or any kind of commercial real estate, is a local market. Remember, in real estate, it is all about location, location, location! Your rental rates are also driven by the competition around you. People who are coming to your community to check it out will also look at two or three other apartment options. For that reason, we use ***www.apartments.com*** a national service which allows apartment hunters to type into a search menu something as simple as, "I want a rental with two bedrooms in Webster, Texas." The site will then show you all the properties within those parameters, and the trick is making sure your property is on the top.

With multifamily properties, each is managed by a separate management company. For any given property, it could be managed by a national company, a local company, or a mom and pop operation. Or, the property could be self-managed, which is what takes place on all of our properties. Moneil Management Group manages all of our owned communities, so we have a much different outlook on how we deal with things and how we make decisions and how quickly we are able to act on things in comparison to other management companies. When too many people are involved from the local level to the district level to the regional level and even to the national level, there can be a lot of red tape.

That was our experience back when I started into this business, ten years or so ago. After thoroughly researching the industry, we hired a very big company out of Dallas. Without naming the company, I can tell you they were really nice people. I knew the owner, the executive vice presidents, and all of their regional managers. At the time, they were managing 33,000 units - just a huge operation. The only problem I had with them was how they were working with the books, the finances in the actual and the accrual basis. Now, that can mess up your cash flow. They would tell me at the end of the month when I would ask about the cash flow, "Cash flow? We don't know because we have paid some bills this month, but there are more bills coming, so we're going to pay them next month. We did collect money this month, but there are some delinquencies, which will be caught up next month."

It was the same problems every month, and they were having difficulties keeping their personnel. And though we were paying them to do it, my partner and I were manning the property...we were in the frontline, actually at the desk, because the company we hired could not keep up

PLATE #5 – ASSET TAKE OVER AND PROPERTY MANAGEMENT · 163

with the community managers. There was so much turnover as employees would come and go. Then the regional managers would come in to hold interviews, and they did not know how to interview, so it was another huge mess.

What we learned in all of that was that each property has its own characteristics, its own personality. Quite simply, there are different rules to follow in different locations or markets and there are different values for each of the various owners. So, as you might expect, each property is unique and must be managed differently than another. We found that no one was as good at managing our properties as the employees we selected and hired into our own property management company.

The only time bad management can work to your advantage is before you buy the property. In your search for just the right property, you will run across those communities that are mismanaged. As syndicators, you want to buy those gold nuggets of mismanaged or poorly managed potential. They have not reached the market rents, and they have not really been optimized. These are the properties where *you* will bring value. We call it "light make-readies" or "upgrades".

Light upgrade is characterized by an expense of about $2500 to $3500 per unit. A deep upgrade is roughly $7500, although there is a range from small to medium to large renovations. When you add granite and tile and lights, along with flooring and molding and all new appliance (all steel, of course) you are bringing deep upgrades to the place. Those upgrades help a lot to bring the value of the property up significantly. When you do those types of things, you can, of course, dictate more rents. Again, every market and every property are unique, but for an example, we might charge $1400 for an upgraded unit, and we even used to charge almost $75 per month to park next to the building in reserved parking spaces. So, you really can dictate your own policies, and they all depend on where you are.

Wherever you are, though, you can always work to REDUCE YOUR PROPERTY TAXES TO INCREASE YOUR CASH FLOW RETURN!

We have all heard the old saying in real estate, "You make your money when you buy," meaning that if you buy it right, it should return a profit. Those of us in the rental business knows that in order to maintain an ongoing profitable return, you need to maximize rent and minimize expenses. By expenses, I am referring to any costs related to the property itself, including, but not limited to, maintenance and repairs costs (including capitalized improvements), hazard and liability insurance premiums, and county property taxes.

By improving the property to market ready condition, you should be able to demand the maximum rent the market will bear. If you rehab the property correctly (meaning don't cut corners), and use quality, durable materials, you will generally keep your maintenance and repair costs to a minimum. By using an insurance vendor that specializes in rental properties, you can be assured of getting the best market rate for the coverage you require. Most investors that I have worked with over the years are already doing these things. What most investors are not doing is reducing their property taxes.

We were very excited about nine years ago when a few companies approached us about helping to reduce our tax burden. We loved the idea, so we negotiated to pay 20% of the savings from our taxes for the year as a fee to one of the companies. In some instances, the savings were several thousand dollars. Some reductions were so significant that they effectively lowered the purchase price of the property. As you are taking over the property as the new owner, the savings here should not be overlooked, as they can significantly increase both monthly cash flow and overall cash-on-cash return with just a couple of hours of work.

PLATE #5 – ASSET TAKE OVER AND PROPERTY MANAGEMENT · 165

Retaining Current Staff on Your New Property

I am often asked about retaining the staff from the former ownership of the property. It is a good question. About a month out from the anticipated closing, it is a good idea to ask the current owner if you can begin interviewing any of his or her staff that has an interest in staying on to work for you under your new LLC (which is unique to each property) and your Property Management Company.

It is important to get the seller's permission before you begin interviewing. Once you do, though, you must interview them as if they were brand new to the business. Conduct reference checks, background checks, and previous employment verifications, which will include the seller from whom you are purchasing the property. Do not assume that because they have been there "forever" that they are good for your business. In fact, we retain very few of the staff members from the properties we acquire.

Remember, most of our deals are for properties that have not reached their full market potential, and oftentimes the employees contribute to that lack of productivity, so we keep very, very few of the former owner's staff in most acquisitions.

For those, we might decide to keep. We offer them a job and include in that offer what we will pay them. It may not be what they were making under the old ownership. Then, they will have the option of accepting our job or rejecting the offer. Either way, we are making plans to manage the property our way and in accordance with our policies and principles. Maybe they can fit into that vision, but most of the time it is simply, "out with the old."

CHAPTER EIGHT

The Syndication Blueprint

Don't buy blindly!

Real estate investors deploy the syndication as an effective tool to turn a good real estate idea into an efficient, money-making venture. If you entertain the idea of achieving success with your idea, the syndication process should be done perfectly. You are, after all, in the same boat with the other investors; you both want to benefit immensely from this process. So, you need to put a flawless syndication in place to enjoy that benefit. To do that, make use of the syndication blueprint.

The syndication blueprint, quite simply, is a detailed analysis of how to make the best use of syndication. The steps are as follows:

1. Get the property under contract

Bringing the property under contract can be done using the following two steps:

Analyze the Property
Your analysis of the property includes the market value, possible renovations and the cost. This will give you an idea of what to present to a potential buyer.

Strike the Right Price and Terms

Keep in mind that buyers seldom pay the asking price for a property. They would rather haggle until both of you arrive at an acceptable price. While haggling with a potential buyer, make sure you have a clear sense of the property's value you determined from your analysis

2. Due Diligence Process

Regardless of the property, you want to buy, whether it is a residential home, an apartment to lease, a commercial business, a skyscraper or a mall, it is very important that you carry out comprehensive due diligence. This will help you to ascertain the quality of the property physically and otherwise. It is very common to hear experts giving professional advice to others by asking them to do their due diligence.

What does this mean?

Doing due diligence is a way to do your homework on a property before you pay for it. You can do this by...

- Performing important calculations
- Taking necessary precautions
- Review important documents

Due diligence also involves walking around the property and procuring insurance for the property. The objective of this process is to determine the value of the property. As you do this, you may spot defects in the structure or other issues that will play a key role in deciding whether to purchase the property or not. If you detect too many issues, you must then consider the potential of significant cost and risk. If those costs and risk are beyond what you can bear, it is advisable to let go of the property.

Carry out the proper due diligence on the property

- Shop the market
- Mortgage financing
- Do the math
- Inspect the property
- Check the insurance

Shop the market

Do not be hasty to buy a property. Many people take the approach of looking at just a couple of properties and purchasing them as soon as they can. That is not ideal. You should take your time to shop the market and look for what suits you before making the purchase. Real estate experts suggest shopping the market for several months before making a purchase. This will offer you the opportunity to purchase a property that will suit your plans.

Mortgage financing

This is another way to make the best of your due diligence. You must have a good knowledge of what the seller wants to offer you here. Anything short of a fair deal that conforms to what other competitors offer is unacceptable. Compare his offer to the offer that others give and decide whether his offer is fair or not. If not, continue to negotiate...or walk away!

Do the math

You must never buy an investment property without doing the math. It is very important for you to pencil down the deal and compare it with other opportunities. How will you ascertain that the deal is good if you don't do that? The advice is: **don't buy blindly**.

Inspect the property

If you are buying a property, you should consider the need to do some minor repairs or renovation. You have to carry out a thorough investigation to determine whether the property is worth your money and investment or not. If you have inspectors, you can bring them in to assist you in assessing and appraising the property. Once your inspector sends you notes on his findings, take your time to go through those notes line by line looking for everything that needs to be repaired or renovated. To have a full grasp of what it will cost you to put the property in a good shape that will satisfy you, you can visit a home repair store and get a quote for what you will repair in the house, using the inspector's or appraiser's remarks as your guide. If you remember that renovating a big property can cost you a small fortune, you will understand why it is important to take this step.

Check the insurance

You must determine whether or not an insurance policy can be written for the property you want to buy. It is important to know how much it will cost you to write an insurance policy, if it is possible, for the property. For example, it is difficult to get a policy for areas that are fire-prone, floods or are susceptible to hurricanes. If you eventually get a policy, it may be too expensive to consider. You should evaluate or count the cost of all of this before you go too far in the process of Underwriting the deal.

Carrying out due diligence on a property should not be overlooked or given less than thorough attention. Completing due diligence will help you to identify some potential risks and rewards associated with a property. You can walk through a property you intend to buy and carry out the property inspection in order to have a general idea of what the property has to offer.

To simplify your work, you may ask the seller for the documents of the property detailing everything about the property. This list should include:

- Information about the current tenants using the property, Rent Roll in excel. Occupancy reports by month for the last two years

- Complete Financial Reports, 12 mo Trailing P&L's for 3-5 years

- The complete uses of the property

- Any inspections or reports by a third party at the order of the seller especially the environmental survey reports

- Surveys of the land

- The current policy of title insurance of the property

- Any condominium documents that apply to it

- Information about any litigation or governmental action about the seller or the estate

- Information about the environmental condition of the estate

- Proof of insurance, loss run report for the last 5 years

- Service contracts

- Any plumbing issues reports

- Any foundation issues reports

- Copies of all the utility bills of the property

- If there is current zoning, the evidence should be included

- All documents relating to construction on the property. This should include all the warranties

You must review the items on the list one after the other. If you cannot do this, let an agent or due diligence professional company do that for you. If there are potential problems, they will be identified. Then… You are investing in a large sum of

Hire an excellent Real Estate and Syndication attorneys!

Investing in real estate is quite challenging, and there are some legal obligations in order to be in control of this process. You must hire excellent real estate and syndication attorney with a good track record. One of the responsibilities of such an attorney is to represent you and/or your company when there are legal issues to be handled. Other areas where you will find the services of an attorney useful are:

- Planning tax
- When you want to construct new projects
- Comply with securities laws
- LLC partnership agreements
- Financing with many lenders
- Check all the adjustments such as unpaid taxes, paid utility costs, and other important things before the closing

Other issues that are handled by the attorney:

Real estate closing: This is also called settlement or completion, and it is the last step taken during a real estate transaction. On the closing date, the owner of the property will transfer the ownership to the buyer. After payment for the property has been completed at the closing, the seller will sign the deed and hand it over to the buyer, in this case, the syndicate. This is where the attorney comes in. The lawyer takes over the transaction and registers the given deed with the land registry office or the deed recorder's office in the county. The attorney must file a declaration about the transaction with the government. The attorney will execute the necessary steps faster and better due to his or her experience in that field. While it is possible for other members of the syndicate to overlook some legal loopholes, an experienced attorney will identify them as he knows what to look for in a document that will prevent future legal tussle.

Purchase agreements: This is an agreement between the seller and the buyer. The attorneys of both the seller and the buyer will be present to serve as witnesses to the signing of an agreement between both parties. This validates the agreement signed by them.

Buy-Sell agreement: The buy-sell agreement is considered by some people as a business will. It is a binding agreement signed by co-owners of a business about what to do if one of the owners of the business dies or has to leave the business for any reason. In the case of syndication, it specifies how to handle the exit of a member of the syndicate. An attorney is needed to validate this agreement, too.

Deeds and registration of title: The property needs to be registered with the government to be considered valid. Having an attorney on hand to go through the deeds before they are registered will give the company immunity to some mistakes that may lead to lawsuits in the future.

Title examination insurance: You need to conduct a title examination on the property before you bid for it. It involves tracing the history of the property, going back to the very first owner. If the property is owned by an LLC, one of the members may be involved in a lawsuit, a state or federal tax lien may be placed on the property, or one of the owners may have experienced foreclosure. An attorney will understand this better and will understand what to do about it to protect you and your investment going forward.

CHAPTER NINE

Motivation & Action Steps

An Investment in knowledge pays the best interest!
— Benjamin Frankin

By now, you have gone through all my five plates, and I hope you have really internalized what it takes to put these syndication packets together. How to find the right deal, the right property, the right real estate investment in the emerging markets. How to underwrite it. How to look at all the numbers. And how to walk away from these investments if they are not right for you.

My INBOX is filled with email from different brokers with whom I have built relationships who are sharing new deals with me. I have to say to many of them that the deals they are bringing are not suitable for my preferred numbers. For that reason, they are not the *right* deals, so I really cannot present them for syndication to my investors.

Overcome Your First Deal Syndrome

Step 1: Put your knowledge to work

- Revisit the material you learned and use it as a guideline
- The knowledge you acquire is powerful

The first thing you must do is put your knowledge to work. Learn the material, check out our university again and again, and look through the bonus material offered at the end of this book. Internalize what you have learned and will learn and make it part of you. Fear and apprehension are to be expected as you get ready to syndicate your first deal. It is uncharted water. Borrowing from the old cliché, I would say to you that knowledge is so powerful. Confidence comes slowly when we understand what we are trying to accomplish, when we understand each and every aspect of trying to do all that we can to gain the investors' interest in our deals.

Step 2: Write down your goals

- Write down your mission statement
- Write down your short-term and long-term plans
- Write down the ACTION STEPS to reach your plans

Having the right mission statement and written goals are so very important. Don't underestimate the value in reading them daily and writing your detailed weekly plan of action. Then, expand on it and make your monthly plan, six-month plan, and twelve- month plan. What small steps must you take to actually reach those plans? That is an important question, the answer to which will lead you to success, which will lead you right back to being primed and ready to syndicate your first deal. I can promise you one thing - once you complete that first deal, one syndication, the second, the third, the tenth, the twentieth will just fall into place. It truly is so easy, and you will find that you keep improving on every single one. It becomes an art. It is like learning as a student how to do it correctly. You put your systems in place, and then you reproduce it again and again. The best part is, when that very first deal is done correctly (and you want to make it the very best it can possibly be), the investors will follow and give you more money, open their wallet more, because they are enjoying all the returns that you proposed to provide them in the PPM, the operating agreement of the entire syndication package.

Step 3: Be Grateful

- You are helping your investors achieve their financial goals putting their money in your deals
- Many people with money want to invest in real estate don't have the knowledge or time to do so

Always demonstrate that attitude of gratitude toward your investors. After all, they are grateful for you, as you are doing something to help them. Your investors are often people who have money but lack the skills or the time to find the kind of great deals in which you are including them. They want to invest in real estate, but perhaps they lack the knowledge, know-how, and means to do so. Doctors, lawyers, and businesspeople are all potential investors. It is amazing how many types of people have so much money in their retirement accounts that they would like to invest. You have the opportunity to teach these people how to bring their money into a self-directed account and then invest with you. So, the attitude of gratitude and doing something to help those people who have money but don't have the skills is very important. We want to really make sure that we are working for the right reason and that we are putting our business together for the right reason with integrity and transparency as we build relationships with investors. Remember, you cannot accomplish your goals by yourself. You will likely become bored, frustrated, and depressed.

Step 4: Build a team

- Choose a business partner(s) and make sure you have the same drive, goals, and aspirations
- Surround yourself with professionals: attorney, broker, CPA, syndication attorney, property managers, etc.

Get one or two or three people, strong people like you who share your desires, goals, aspirations, integrity, and attitude. Together, you will be able to pull one another up when somebody's down, possess a wealth of collective knowledge about real estate, share the duties of the syndication, and be able to challenge and motivate each other. So, have faith! Remember it's always achievable because, if others have done it, and many of them have, why not you? Have that attitude. That is so very important! And trust that things will work out for the best. They really will. They always do. I have encountered every frustration in my career in real estate, but we kept on and kept on, and every day was a new day. Every challenge was a new challenge. We knew we would figure out a way to accomplish our dream, to reach the end result.

Step 5: Continue your education

- It is important to continuously learn and improve
- Have a mentor who will guide you

Another important piece of the puzzle for getting past the first deal syndrome is to get a coach! Get a coach. It is so important to have that person with experience to whom you can sound off your ideas. Share with your coach what you are looking into, what kind of properties you are considering. Seek your coach's input on whether or not they are good investments. Our success really comes from this one idea because it moved us from a very small position to a very strong path really quickly, and it allowed us to build a solid foundation because coaches are the ones who have already done these kinds of things, and they can challenge you and think through the deals with you and give you the ideas that you may or may not have thought about.

Step 6: Learn how to syndicate

- This will set the path for your financial freedom

Syndication is a process; it is a system; it is an art. And I hope you will take time to learn it to the fullest and happily pursue lots of investors to be involved in your deals as you put them together.

As we consider the importance of attitude, drive, dedication, and passion, you must ask yourself, "What will it take to put my first deal together? My second? My third? Fourth? Tenth in syndication?" What is the attitude and level of dedication you need to achieve the results you hope for?

It's the DESIRE within an individual to excel against all odds that steers them towards accomplishing their goals!

The Drive to Achieve

How do you define the phrase *drive to achieve*? *Drive to achieve* is the desire within an individual to excel against any odds and to reach designated goals, the goals that you have set up, the written-down goals, the end result you seek. We just have to work harder and work through things above, over, and beyond everything - against all odds - to reach the designated goals. That is the drive. That's dedication!

Dedication

Dedication is *the quality of a sole commitment to a task or purpose*! So, let's ask the question: what's the real reason you are in syndication business? What is the reason that you are drawn to this book? What is your level of dedication? How committed are you? All of this will correlate directly to how quickly and how easily you will achieve results.

Passion

Passion is one of the most powerful engines of success. When you do a thing, put your whole soul into it; step into it with your own personality. Be active, be energetic, and be faithful, and you will accomplish your object.

> *"Nothing great was ever achieved without passion."*
> *– Ralph Waldo Emerson*

This really great quote from Ralph Waldo Emerson really echoes for us because for us to achieve success, we must be reading, listening, and spending time with the people who are successful. You must read the books and listen to the podcasts and go to the universities (like ours) and seek knowledge so that you can really make a difference in your thinking process and grow stronger each day in the pursuit of your dream. I believe in the challenge of accomplishing something extraordinary out of the plain and ordinary.

Let me confess, I came here about 38 years ago, and I could not even speak English. I was an engineer back in India, in Bombay. I came to the U.S. to gain my master's in business administration. I said in my heart, "I am going to learn." My accent was heavy, and people were not able to understand me. So, I really took the goal of achieving success to heart, and I started reading great books.

I recommend them to you. Books like *Life is Tremendous,* by Charlie Tremendous Jones. I still have a copy after 40 years. I read Zig Ziglar, Napoleon Hill, Dale Carnegie, John Maxwell, Robert Kiyosaki, Eckhart Tolle, Wayne Dyer, Tom Hopkins, Jim Rohn, Tony Robbins, and Steven Covey's books. If you haven't read Covey's *Seven Habits of Highly Effective People,* I highly recommend that you read it (after you finish reading my book, of course). Books like Covey's really came in handy in shaping our attitude and making sure that every day is a productive one for us.

Make it a Habit

- Not to procrastinate
- Work diligently
- Keep a clear focus
- Have a clear purpose – FOCUS is KEY!
- Be optimistic – maintain a positive attitude
- Work hard – 98% of achievement comes from this
- Learn continuously

Today is a gift to us, and we waste it if it is not lived to the fullest. Enjoy that gift! Be better and learn and achieve more with each new day.

Don't procrastinate! Procrastination kills lots of great ideas and plans and dreams and goals. Procrastination is the biggest fatal disease in this business. I say move fast, learn as much as you can, and enjoy every day. You must be working diligently each and every day to move forward.

You must have a clear direction. The future may be made up of many uncertainties, but be passionate in your work, and not only will you survive, but you will thrive. Clarity of focus is so important. Ambiguity is the enemy of change. We don't change from one day to the next. Instead, we live our lives with pleasure and pain. The key is to leverage that pain to help ensure going forward that you can enjoy the lifestyle and the passive incomes that go hand in hand with helping achieve their goals and dreams. That's what you want to really put your efforts into.

What is the purpose? What is the clarity of vision behind all this work, this whole project of syndication? Is the sun shining where you are? If so, take a magnifying glass in your hand, go outside, and hold it in one hand. With your other hand, make a fist. Now, moving that magnifying glass toward the sun, let the light penetrating it pinpoint a spot on the back side of your fisted hand. Hold it there a minute.... but not too long. When the whole energy of the sun passes through the glass is concentrated into one dot, guess what? The back of the fist is going to start burning. That's the power of focus. When clarity and focus are present, things get accomplished.

Be an optimist. The golden rule is to maintain a positive attitude and always believe in yourself. Being an optimist does not simply mean seeing the brighter side of life; it means dealing with your circumstances by maximizing your strengths and achievements rather than focusing and being limited by your weaknesses and apprehensions. Every problem has a solution if only we develop the attitude that we are going to go to the top - beyond that 100% mark when we really need to go even a little bit further. It's our attitude towards life and work that drives us to live beyond that 100% mark.

Procrastination: How to Kick the Habit

There is a tug of war that's happening within you. On one side, there's a part of you that wants to get things done. On the opposite side, there's that part of you that's in the habit of delaying important tasks.

There's no doubt that procrastination is a productivity killer, but it's also a normal occurrence. Still, it's a problem worth addressing, especially if it interferes with your performance at work.

If you continuously ignore important tasks, then you have a bad case of procrastination. The consequence of this is that you are unable to achieve short-term goals. This, in turn, makes it impossible for you to achieve long-term goals.

There are various reasons why people procrastinate. It could be that they see the task as too difficult or too easy. Either way, we will have to take action if we want to achieve greater success in life.

Here are the four important strategies to keep in mind when addressing procrastination.

1. Accept that you're procrastinating

Having too many expectations is one of the signs that you're procrastinating. Basically, procrastinators search for reasons to delaying an important task. What's worse is that they deny the fact that they're procrastinating. On that note, the first step to resolving procrastination is to simply become aware of the habit and its effects.

2. Know why are you procrastinating

Understanding the main reason why you're procrastinating is essential before facing the problem. Basically, the problem could have originated from a feeling of fear. Due to the demands of a certain task, you feel like holding back. You worry that you may not do well at it. If that's the case, then you will need to focus on developing a more confident mindset. When you determine the problem earlier, it will be easier for you to address it.

If you find yourself procrastinating, you will need to know what's causing you to delay your tasks. You will then have better clarity in making positive changes to your habits.

3. Discipline and motivate yourself

Procrastination is part of one's behavioral pattern. This would mean that it can be avoided given that the right approaches are applied. Discipline is key here, so it pays to be strict with yourself. For this, you can focus on the rewards you will be getting. You should also realize that there are consequences if you fail to complete these tasks.

4. Focus on building your mindset

A focused life starts in the mind. In fact, it's impossible to even think of making positive changes without being in the right mindset. A little motivation goes a long way, so you should keep on reminding yourself that you can do it. There's nothing to stop you if you just believe that you can finish a task on time.

These four simple steps should help you overcome procrastination. It's important to keep into mind that you can hurdle any barrier if you have the strength and the spirit that can make things possible!

Ways to Nurturing Your Mindset for Success

Everybody wants a successful life, don't they? I've always wanted that, too. It's possible when we nurture a positive mindset that will result in a better and fruitful outlook in life. Let's have an illustration of what it looks like.

Let's view the concept of a mindset as a dartboard. Our goals are the rings. In order to hit our targets, we need precision, which usually takes constant practice and focus. That being said, let me show you how you can nurture your mindset for success.

Determine your goals and develop a clear mind

The first thing we need to do is to determine the specific goals we want to accomplish. Second, we need to know which goals to prioritize. After that, we can focus on our goals by having a clear and calm mindset. Apart from that, we also need to have sufficient self-confidence and flexibility in making decisions. This can only be possible if we flush out all the negative thoughts that are lingering inside our heads. Doing so will allow us to nurture a goal-oriented mindset.

As Confucius once said, "He that would perfect his work must first sharpen his tools." No doubt, our minds are our best tools and it's important to keep it fine-tuned.

Surround yourself with positivity

You can get a lot of benefits when you're developing a mindset that's anchored on positivity. One thing's for sure, you become more confident in addressing the daily challenges you face. Other than that, the benefits of positivity can impact your well-being. You begin to lead a healthier lifestyle if you let positive thoughts influence your outlook.

The positive mindset that you have can also impact the people that surround you. After all, if there's something you want to share, it's your perspective in life. So, start by talking to your friends and family. Be confident and optimistic because you will make a big impact on the lives of the people who are close to you.

Failures are your life's lessons

Mistakes, mistakes, mistakes! Everyone makes mistakes, so you don't have to feel bad if think you have done a terrible job. If anything, you're still far away from failing. That said, you should never treat your mistakes like they are the worst thing that could ever happen to you. Instead, you can treat these as lessons you can learn from.

One thing's for sure, these negative experiences will make us think from a broader perspective. As a result, we become more effective in dealing with similar situations in the future.

You've aimed and shot well

Now that you have perfected the game of darts, it's only a matter of applying what you have learned. You now have the mindset of a champion, one who would never quit no matter the odds.

As you win one game after another, you may as well keep the momentum going. Continue striving and reaching out for bigger rewards. If you really desire more achievements, you'll be ready this time around because you're already equipped with the best mindset.

I truly hope that you have learned lots of great ideas, techniques and strategies to understand the Art of Syndication Investing in Commercial Real Estate; especially in Multifamily or Apartments. I know that you have come a long way before you picked this book up. Do you feel empowered?

I have tried my best to communicate the very principles I learned over 14 years and have implemented with a positive attitude, passion, vision, and hard work.

Call to Action (CTA)

Well what's next?

I sincerely hope that are highly motivated to learn more about this "life changing art of syndication" for investing in commercial real estate I know that the art of syndication has changed my life!! And I truly hope that learning the principles and the practice that I have put in place for you will change yours!!

About three years back, I started coaching and mentoring all levels of interested investors who wanted to learn this very art of syndication. I started to record the video and audio lectures as I was repeating myself again and again to make students understand the concepts. Understandably, I was getting tired and overwhelmed of constant repetition. After recording over 550 lectures, I have been able to put together one of the top academies in the nation. I will let you be the judge.

As a special "Thank You" gift, I would like to give you a $500 discount coupon to redeem at my www.VinneyChopra.com/Academy

Thanks again for investing in this book, I look forward to getting to know you and welcome your feedback on this book on Amazon or directly to my team and I by sending your feedback to

info@multifamilyAcademy.com

or on www.apartmentsyndicationmadeeasy.com

I look forward to adding more value to your life changing, syndication journey and I am excited to see my students become just as successful as I am, maybe even more!!! You have a leg up from me, I never was able to access such comprehensive material when I started to syndicate! Remember it can be done by climbing step by step just like I did!

I will see you in the Academy. If you are serious investor, do take a look at it and apply for Mentorship!!

About Vinney Chopra

When Vinney Chopra came to the United States from India more than 40 years ago, he had only $7 in his pockets. But he knew without a doubt that the opportunities offered by this country were within reach because he had a vision for his life, plus the commitment to learn, work hard and sacrifice to achieve those goals.

With a bachelor's degree in mechanical engineering, he entered George Washington University to seek a Master of Business Administration degree in marketing and advertising. He sold Bibles and educational books door-to-door to support his studies, excelling both in the classroom and outside because of his work ethic and overwhelmingly positive attitude.

There's a reason Vinney's nickname is "Mr. Smiles," which is evident even through just hearing the demeanor in his voice! He has always believed in individuals' ability to shape the world around them through positive thought and selfless actions, and he has been a passionate motivational speaker and teacher for over three decades. After getting a taste of sales and marketing while pursuing his MBA, Vinney decided to leave engineering altogether and become a motivational speaker and fundraiser. He worked tirelessly to build a clientele that would work with him annually to raise the funds to meet their goals and dreams.

To learn more about Vinney, visit www.VinneyChopra.com

Made in the
USA
Columbia, SC